OECD Anti-Spam Toolkit of Recommended Policies and Measures

OECD

ORGANISATION FOR ECONOMIC CO-OPERATION AND DEVELOPMENT

ORGANISATION FOR ECONOMIC CO-OPERATION AND DEVELOPMENT

The OECD is a unique forum where the governments of 30 democracies work together to address the economic, social and environmental challenges of globalisation. The OECD is also at the forefront of efforts to understand and to help governments respond to new developments and concerns, such as corporate governance, the information economy and the challenges of an ageing population. The Organisation provides a setting where governments can compare policy experiences, seek answers to common problems, identify good practice and work to co-ordinate domestic and international policies.

The OECD member countries are: Australia, Austria, Belgium, Canada, the Czech Republic, Denmark, Finland, France, Germany, Greece, Hungary, Iceland, Ireland, Italy, Japan, Korea, Luxembourg, Mexico, the Netherlands, New Zealand, Norway, Poland, Portugal, the Slovak Republic, Spain, Sweden, Switzerland, Turkey, the United Kingdom and the United States. The Commission of the European Communities takes part in the work of the OECD.

OECD Publishing disseminates widely the results of the Organisation's statistics gathering and research on economic, social and environmental issues, as well as the conventions, guidelines and standards agreed by its members.

• • •

The Toolkit was declassified on 29 March 2006 by the ICCP committee and the CCP, and the Enforcement Recommendation was adopted by the Council at its meeting on 13 April 2006. The Task Force's mandate ends in June 2006.

The work of the Task Force was supported by financial voluntary contributions from Australia, Canada, the Czech Republic, Italy, and Norway.

The work of the Task Force was supported by Dimitri Ypsilanti and Claudia Sarrocco of the OECD Secretariat.

Also available in French under the title:
Boîte à outils anti-spam de l'OCDE : Politiques et mesures recommandées

FOREWORD

In view of the potential for economic and social harm of spam, and the potential for further problems as a result of the convergence of communication technologies, the ICCP Committee, in consultation with the Committee on Consumer Policy, endorsed in April 2004 the proposal for the creation of a horizontal *ad hoc* "Task Force on Spam" to assist in the further conduct and co-ordination of the work on spam and obtain a more rapid consensus on a policy framework to tackle spam issues. The creation of the Task Force on Spam, as a joint subsidiary body of these Committees, was approved by the OECD Council.

The OECD Anti-Spam Toolkit was developed in the framework of the OECD Task Force on Spam and includes a package of recommended policies and measures addressing regulatory approaches, enforcement co-operation, industry driven activities, technical solutions, education and awareness initiatives, spam measures, and international co-operation and exchange.

This document comprises an executive summary, which synthesizes the Toolkit recommended policies and measures and the Task Force Report, divided into eight main sections representing the elements listed above. It is completed by the OECD Council Recommendation on cross-border co-operation in the enforcement of laws against spam; the BIAC and MAAWG Best Practices on ISPs and Network operators; and the BIAC Best Practices for Email Marketing. In the annexes are also available the Spam Referral proforma, contributed by the CNSA/LAP, and the Mobile Spam Code of Practice, elaborated in the framework of the GSM Association.

The Anti-Spam Toolkit is also available online, together with background resources and materials, updated information on countries' spam laws and a list of national focal points for enforcement authorities. The website is online at **www.oecd-antispam.org**.

TABLE OF CONTENTS

Figures

Boxes

EXECUTIVE SUMMARY

In view of the wide impact of spam, and the potential for further problems as a result of the convergence of communication technologies and the emergence of ubiquitous communications and mobile Internet, the OECD brought together policy makers and industry experts to form the **OECD Task Force on Spam** (hereinafter, the "Task Force"). They were charged with developing a framework aimed at tackling spam using a broad multi-disciplinary range of solutions.

The Task Force developed the **Anti-Spam Toolkit** (the "Toolkit"), which recommends a range of policies and measures which should be key elements of a comprehensive public policy framework for addressing the problem of spam. These policies and measures are summarised below.

Status and evolution of spam

In order for electronic communication platforms, applications and services to contribute to economic and social development, they must be reliable, efficient and trustworthy. Today, however, e-mail and other electronic communication tools may be threatened by unsolicited, unwanted, and harmful electronic messages, commonly known as spam. Unless these threats are curtailed, they could erode users' trust and confidence.

Spam, which began as electronic messages usually advertising commercial products or services, has evolved over the past few years, and to simple advertising messages have been added messages that are potentially dangerous, which can be deceptive, may cause network disruptions, may result in some form of fraud and which are used as a vehicle for spreading viruses and other malware.

A consistent and co-ordinated approach to spam

There is not a simple solution to stop spam. The openness and decentralised nature of the Internet, which are the main reasons for its success, have also created the conditions leading to a number of vulnerabilities that are increasingly exploited by spammers and other online offenders. The lack of centralised control enables users to hide their identity. In addition, the low cost of accessing Internet and e-mail services allows spammers to send out millions of spam messages every day at an extremely low marginal cost so that only a small response rate is required to attain high profits. However, in combating spam and other online threats it is viewed as important to maintain the openness, flexibility and innovation underlying the Internet.

In this context, the Task Force, at the beginning of its mandate, had to decide on the appropriate action to take and the roles of the different stake-holders in fighting spam. There was consensus that Governments should work to establish clear national anti-spam policies in concert with other players, collaborate with the private sector, and promote co-operation across borders. It was also agreed that to fight spam it was important to set up domestic co-ordination groups, and create appropriate regulatory frameworks, based on well-defined policy objectives and backed by effective enforcement mechanisms. It was recognised that the private sector has the lead role for the development of relevant business practices and innovative technical solutions, and can greatly contribute to the education of users. Co-ordination and co-operation among public and private players is critical to eradicating spam.

In this context, the OECD Task Force on Spam developed the concept of an Anti-Spam Toolkit, with the objective to provide OECD members with a comprehensive policy orientation and consistent framework in their fight against spam. There was a conviction that this framework would also be applicable and useful for non-OECD countries. The Toolkit is composed of eight inter-related elements, addressing:

Regulatory approaches: The development of anti-spam legislation that tackles spam and related problems is fundamental. Legislation should set clear directions on what is allowed and what is not allowed.

Enforcement concerns: While having the appropriate legislation is indeed necessary, implementation and application of the law is fundamental. The timeliness and speed in taking enforcement action and applying sanctions is crucial, if spam is to be effectively curbed, and traditional enforcement procedures which can take several weeks or months are not fully effective in the online world. Particular attention in the context of spam should be given to national co-ordination, sanctions, empowerment of enforcement authorities, and cross-border enforcement co-operation.

Industry driven initiatives: In order to appropriately deal with spam, domestic anti-spam laws should be coupled with private sector initiatives.

Technical solutions: Anti-spam tools operate at many levels – at the point of origination of e-mail, in the backbone network, at the gateway and on the recipient computer – and may be used alone or in combination. Any attempt to combat spam effectively must involve the sensible application and administration of a number of these technological tools and methods. No method will be entirely successful in isolation. When a number of anti-spam technologies are effectively used in collaboration with one another, they can drastically reduce the level of spam affecting a system.

Education and awareness: A comprehensive anti-spam strategy must ensure that the end-user, who is the final recipient of spam, the possible victim of viruses and scams, and, at the same time, the person who has control over their computer and personal information, is sufficiently educated and aware of how to deal with spam and other online threats. Education and awareness-raising activities are needed in large enterprises, small and medium-sized enterprises, for residential users and in education establishments. They must aim to create a culture of security, and encourage a responsible use of cyberspace.

Co-operative partnerships against spam: There is a common interest by public and private players in preserving the availability and reliability of communication tools to promote the development of the digital economy. Public-private sector co-operation is taking place in a number of innovative ways. The objectives of strategic partnerships are usually awareness raising activities and information sharing. More operational partnerships also contribute to education, development (and application) of best practices and exchange of information and data on cross-border spam cases. In addition, as seen from the efforts occurring at national and international levels, partnerships are a fundamental tool for improving communication and better understanding reciprocal needs, expectations and problems, and therefore enhance co-operation and mutual involvement.

Spam metrics: Measurement is key to evaluating the evolution of spam and the effectiveness of anti-spam solutions and educational efforts. The metrics allow the evaluation of national strategies and their implementation and provide insights into what changes are needed in policy, regulatory and technical frameworks.

Global co-operation (Outreach): Spam, like the Internet, knows no borders, and travels from and to developed and developing economies. In this context, global co-operation is fundamental to promote appropriate domestic frameworks to counter spam in all countries, and to encourage co-operation among governments, private sector, civil society and other stakeholders. Co-operation is needed to ensure the harmonized and widespread application of technical measures and the effective enforcement of applicable rules.

For each of the above elements, the Task Force recommended a number of policies and practices:

Element I. Regulatory approaches

The development of anti-spam legislation which tackles spam and related problems is fundamental.

National anti-spam regulation should attempt to:

Preserve the benefits of electronic communications by increasing user trust in the Internet and electronic messaging media and improve the availability, reliability and efficiency of services, as well as the performance of global communication networks.

Prohibit and take action against the act of spamming, as defined by national law. Legislation alone may not stop potential spammers from taking advantage of this marketing technique, however laws and regulations can have an impact by sanctioning against those individuals and organizations that choose to make use of spam and profit from it. The value of legislation will depend on sanctions, in particular in the certainty of their application.

Reduce the amount of spam. To prevent spam from being sent, activities need to be targeted at different stages, in order to reduce the volume of spam traversing networks, and reduce the number of spam received by end-users.

To achieve these goals, legislation should conform to four general principles:

Policy direction: The legislation should provide a clear policy direction. The main lines and objectives of national and international anti-spam policy should be outlined at an earlier stage and need to underlie the entire governmental strategy.

Regulatory simplicity: The legislation should be short and simple.

Enforcement effectiveness: Enforcement is a fundamental issue, which, if not dealt with appropriately, can make a good piece of legislation useless. For this reason it is important to put in place an effective sanction regime and appropriate standards of proof. In addition, appropriate powers and resources need to be allocated for enforcement authorities.

International linkages: As spam is a cross-border issue, legislation should foresee appropriate international linkages, and provide national authorities with the possibility to co-operate in investigations and exchange information with foreign authorities (see below).

In reviewing best practices for legislation, the following elements should be included as far as possible, taking into account a country's institutional and legal framework:

	Issues	**Approach**
Scope	Services concerned	Messaging format will merge or evolve, and unforeseen messaging media may arise. Two possible legislative approaches can be adopted: "Technology specific": Target specific messaging technologies, usually those that pose a current spam problem. "Technology neutral": The regulatory instrument covers communication technologies in general, and is sufficiently flexible to encompass future changes in messaging technology without needing amendment. Real-time voice to voice services could be separately regulated.
Scope	Commercial purpose	Consider whether legislation should only address commercial and transactional messages, or whether it should also address specific non-commercial content, such as political or religious messages. Specific categories of messages can be expressly excluded from the scope of the law (e.g. messages from academic institutions to their alumni).
Consent	Consent	The degree of consent or permission which legislators or regulators wish to require may vary depending on the approach to spam regulation. There are three major approaches to consent, which are often blended in the legislation: Expressed: form of consent where an individual or organisation has actively given their permission to a particular action or activity (opt-in). Inferred/implicit: consent which generally can be inferred from the conduct and/or other business relationships of the recipient. Assumed consent: there is a presumption of consent until it is removed by the recipient, for example by "unsubscribing" (opt-out).

	Issues	Approach
Requirements for legitimate marketing message	Unsubscribe address	Messages should always include a functional opt-out facility, which allows the recipient to unsubscribe by indicating their wish not to receive in future further communications from the sending party. This implies that a valid return address has to be included in e-mail, so that the recipient may easily unsubscribe. A postal address could also be required. The lack of an opt-out facility, the absence of a valid return address and valid postal address, or the failure to cease the transmission of the messages within the period of time established by the law should be sanctioned.
	Information about message origins	A key challenge in the regulation of spamming and the enforcement of spam laws is to respond to the ability of spammers to obfuscate the origin of spam being sent: • Legislation needs to prohibit the sending of e-mails which falsify the origin or conceal header/ID information. • Legislation should also require that the marketer supporting the sender of e-mail should be clearly identified.
	Not bulk	Legislation may foresee that e-mail is classified as spam only if a certain number of messages have been sent in a given period of time (usually over 50-100 over 24 hours). This element of course needs to take into account the fact that there is legitimate bulk e-mail (e.g. newsletters, etc.).
	Labelling	Legislation may include a provision requiring the use of a specific label for e-mail containing advertising, pornographic material, etc.
Ancillary elements	Person authorising the sending of the spam or aiding/assisting the spammer	The law should not sanction only the person physically sending the message, but also the person who commissioned or authorised the messages to be sent or who has gained financially through spamming activities. This approach could facilitate enforcement, as it is often difficult to determine who actually sent the spam while it may be easier to determine the marketer benefiting from spamming activity.
	Harvesting software and harvested address lists Dictionary attacks	Legislation may include specific provisions to levy additional sanctions if such tools are used to aid the sending of spam in contravention of the jurisdiction's spam legislation: the act of selling, acquiring or using harvesting software or harvested address lists, or the automatic generation of recipients' addresses may be sanctioned.

	Issues	Approach
Cybercrimes and content-related questions	Illegal access	Legislation should forbid the unauthorised use of protected computer resources. Anybody compromising computers in order to use them to send messages should be sanctioned.
	Misleading or fraudulent content	Focus on the content of the message. This leaves aside many of the systemic concerns regarding spam messages. Spam scams and phishing could constitute computer-related offences, i.e. ordinary crimes that are frequently committed through the use of a computer system. • Anti-spam legislation could include provisions on prohibiting misleading or deceptive subject heading, in addition. • Spam legislation may cover the content of messages, in particular if anti-fraud laws, consumer protection legislation, etc. are not clearly drawn out.
	Security threats	*Malware* aspects of spam are often criminalised by statute or can be criminalised using the Council of Europe Convention on Cybercrime framework.
International element	Cross-border jurisdiction	Regulation should: • Specify that messages sent to or from the jurisdiction are covered, as well as messages commissioned from within the jurisdiction and financial benefits linked with spam. • Spammers who operate from national jurisdiction, even though they spam other countries, should be sanctioned by domestic legislation. • Domestic enforcement authorities should be empowered to undertake international co-operation and cross-border enforcement agreements are important.

The role of Internet Service Providers and e-mail service providers is also important, and could be considered in legislation. In particular: governments and regulators should support the development of ISP codes of practice that complement and are consistent with legislation. Governments should encourage industry associations to develop such codes and adopt best practices where they are in the public interest and do not impose undue financial and administrative burdens on participants. Annexes II and III of the Toolkit provide a best practice agreement developed by the Business and Industry Advisory Committee (BIAC) and the Messaging Anti-Abuse Working Group (MAAWG) in the context of the work by the Task Force on Spam.

Such codes, according to national practices and legislative provisions, could also be registered with the national enforcement agency where appropriate. This registration could enable the authority to require an industry participant to comply with the code in case the industry association does not succeed in doing so.

Legislation could also provide a comprehensive framework to support the activities of ISPs to block or limit the circulation of spam e-mail. ISPs should be able to take appropriate and balanced defensive measures to protect their networks, and should be allowed to take legal action against spammers. Similar results could be achieved through appropriate contractual provisions between ISPs and users.

Element II. Enforcement

Legislation needs to ensure that enforcement agencies have adequate powers in order to function effectively. Following the proposal of the Spam Task Force an **OECD Council Recommendation on Spam Cross-Border Enforcement Co-operation** (Annex I) has been agreed to. On the basis of the recommendation, governments should improve their legislation in order to:

a) Establish a domestic framework of laws, enforcement authorities, and practices for the enforcement of anti-spam legislation.

b) Improve the ability of authorities to co-operate with their foreign counterparts, providing national bodies with the possibility to share relevant information and provide investigative assistance.

c) Improve procedures for co-operation, prioritising requests for assistance and making use of common resources and networks.[1]

d) Develop new co-operative models between enforcement authorities and relevant private sector entities.

Element III. Industry-driven initiatives

In order to appropriately deal with spam, generally-applicable anti-spam laws should be coupled with self-regulatory initiatives undertaken by private sector players, such as Internet Service Providers and e-mail service providers, telecommunication operators, direct marketers, online operators, software companies, and their associations.

Private sector initiatives are an important part of the policy framework. The Task Force:

- Welcomes the efforts made by BIAC and MAAWG in drafting best practices and notes the results achieved so far.
- Encourages their continued development, including through dialogue with appropriate policy and regulatory bodies.
- Notes that best practices will evolve in light of regulatory, technical and commercial developments.
- Notes that in some jurisdictions there is scope for formal recognition of such best practices.

Providers of online services and goods should, in carrying out their activities, take action to develop:

- Corporate communication methods and standards which respect the privacy of their customers, carefully managing personal information and e-mail addresses. Company standards for Web sites, domain usage and e-mail messaging help protect users. Clear company e-mail policies – such as never asking for personal information or possibly never providing a clickable link in an e-mail – should be established and applied consistently. A company sending out e-mail to its customers may consider the possibility to authenticate them or use digital signatures.

- Pre-emptive activities to create barriers to e-mail scams such as phishing should be considered. These include measures to make the company's Web site less vulnerable to brand attacks by using clear domain name and defensive domain registration (*e.g.* register domain names which are similar to the company's own domain and may create confusion), Web site usage monitoring, control of "bounced" messages, monitoring of look-alike sites, etc.

- Consumer education and awareness, customer support. Online operators should communicate effectively with their customers. They should clarify which kind of communications can/will be sent by e-mail, define how e-mail addresses and other information may be accessed and modified by the user, specify that the user will never be asked to provide their personal data via e-mail, and list elements users need to verify in the message to be sure it is from the online operator.

Direct marketers should:

- Adopt and effectively implement a code of conduct using best practices for electronic marketing, which include marketing messages sent by e-mail, instant messaging, or mobile. These associations, as well as associations of online operators, could have stricter relationships with ISPs and other network operators, to reduce the number of false positives, while at the same time guaranteeing the legitimacy and fairness of their activities.

- Adopt best practices or codes of conduct that should aim at facilitating and complementing the application of anti-spam legislation, at national and international levels. For this reason appropriate information about different legislative approaches should be provided by governments and associations.

The OECD Task Force notes that BIAC has developed a set of recommended best practices for e-mail marketing, attached as Annex III to this report.

Internet Service Providers and other network operators should:

- Adopt and effectively implement self-regulation in the form of best practices and codes of conduct.

- Adopt and enforce Acceptable Use Policy (AUPs), which will forbid spamming, and related activities on their networks. These policies would be part of a contractual agreement between the provider and the user where their violation would result in a breach of contract, and allow the suspension of service and termination of the contract.

- Provide subscribers information about the availability, use and appropriate application of software for filtering spam and viruses. Filtering solutions and updates should be provided at a reasonable price, and links to open source anti-spam and anti-virus software should be indicated to users.

Governments should encourage national ISPs and other network operators to adopt and effectively implement recommended best common practices. The OECD notes the recommended best practices for ISPs and other network operators which have been developed by BIAC and MAAWG and are available in Annex II of this report.

Mobile operators should adopt and effectively implement measures to reduce spam on their networks. The range of new services offered over mobile phone creates new spam-like problems for mobile users. Mobile operator measures should include contractual, technical and educational tools. The OECD Task Force notes the GSM Association best practices for mobile operators, which are attached to this report as Annex IV.

Element IV. Technical measures

Internet Service Providers and other network operators should constantly improve their knowledge and operating practices, and update their technical best practices, such as best practices for ISPs and other network operators mentioned in Element III, in order to face new challenges and technological evolution and promote the implementation and sharing of available technical solutions among providers. When a number of anti-spam technologies are effectively used in collaboration with one another, the effect can be to drastically reduce the level of spam impacting a system. Although important in reducing the volume of spam in inboxes, filtering by itself is insufficient to reduce the volume of spam originating on different networks so that a range of technical solutions need to be implemented to achieve effective protection.

Element V. Education and awareness initiatives

Individual users:

- Governments should:
  - Develop public information and awareness campaigns to educate end-users as to the products and services they are using and the associated risks they may face, thus allowing users to protect themselves from spam, viruses and other malicious codes. This information should be made available also on ISPs portals.
  - Organise nation-wide campaigns to attract the attention of the media and the population at large.
  - Work with the private sector, civil society and other interested parties on user education campaigns initiatives.
- Given their ability to reach individual users on the Web, ISPs and other network operators, including mobile operators, should use their company-customer communication channels (Web site, portals, sms, newsletters) to provide information to their customers on:
  - How to avoid spam and risks connected with spam e-mails, SMS, MMS, etc.
  - Available anti-spam and anti-virus filters, open source solutions for the concerned platform.
  - Indications on how to report spam abuses to the ISPs or the user's operator and to competent authorities, and
  - E-mail/phone contact to the provider's abuse desk.

Users' groups:

Computer classes for **senior citizens**, possibly financed by the government or local authorities, should include information on computer security, and practical examples on how to avoid spam, online frauds, viruses and other malicious software.

Awareness of online threats and security issues should be part of **students' and children's** computer classes. Cartoons and comics could also be used to reach out to young users.

Large companies and SMEs:

- **Companies:** IT support should make available to new staff a pamphlet explaining the company's security policy for e-mail, existing filters and best practices for dealing with spam and how to avoid being spammed. The same kind of information should be available on the internal Web site, and updates should be sent to users periodically.

- **Small medium-sized enterprises:** Commercial associations, ISPs and security software companies should provide SMEs specific information on simplified security management practices, training material, free open source software, etc. Examples and resource materials are available on the OECD Task Force Website at www.oecd-antispam.org.

The education of recipients is as important as the education of senders. Regulators and business associations can play an important role in educating companies by disseminating information on how business can communicate with their clients using electronic messaging, such as e-mail, in a manner that complies with national legislation.

Direct marketing associations should inform their members of relevant anti-spam legislation in force in their country of origin and in the country of destination of the message. Online marketing best practices and informational WebPages should be developed and co-ordinated at the international level.

Element VI. Co-operative partnerships

Any anti-spam strategy should be developed and implemented in the context of public-private partnerships, with participation of representatives from the public and from the private sectors. Anti-spam measures will only be effective if the full range of players is involved in their elaboration, accept them (and their side-effects) and consider them appropriate to respond to their needs.

Recommended best practices, developed by industry associations, with the input of public authorities, should be adopted widely. Such best practices should be widely disseminated and implemented. They should also be updated where appropriate to take into account a changing technological and service environment (see also Element 3).

Industry and enforcement authorities should co-operate in the enforcement of anti-spam legislation. In particular, ISPs and other network operators should be in contact with the authorities to signal possible cases of spam, and should be allowed to share with the same bodies information on spam activities in their network.

Element VII. Spam metrics

Governments and private sector players should monitor the impact of anti-spam measures, to assess their effectiveness. ISPs, other network operators, and national anti-spam agencies should, to the extent possible, share information and data on the intensity and scope of spam and its evolution. Measuring methods should be detailed and documented, in order to improve the legibility of the results obtained. In this context MAAWG developed its Email Metrics Program. The Task Force welcomes this initiative and encourages its continuation and development.

Element VIII. Global co-operation

The Task Force on Spam recommends that the Toolkit and the best practices noted in the present document should be made widely available to non-OECD economies as well as within OECD countries and its resources should be accessible to the largest possible number of people. In this context a web site has been developed by the Task Force, and is available at www.oecd-antispam.org. In order for the website to continue to be a useful and up to date resource, countries are urged to regularly provide contributions, new material, and news on their national anti-spam initiatives.

OECD member countries should promote and facilitate anti-spam activities in other countries, through partnerships – bilateral or multilateral arrangements, information sharing, etc. – in order to help in the development of appropriate anti-spam legislation, support the implementation of technical solutions and the diffusion of educational tools and resources.

INTRODUCTION

Spam is having a negative impact on the digital economy, and results in important economic and social costs for OECD and non-OECD countries. Given the potential for further problems as a result of the convergence of communication technologies and the emergence of ubiquitous communication and mobile Internet, OECD member countries are faced with the necessity of finding effective ways to combat spam. In order to meet this challenge, the OECD's Committee for Information, Computer and Communications Policy (ICCP) at its meeting on 3-4 March 2003 supported work on this important topic, requesting that it be placed on a fast track, and noting that this was a global issue. The Committee on Consumer Policy (CCP) also expressed interest in pursuing OECD work on this topic. An initial exploration of issues linked with spam was undertaken in a background document and in a Workshop on Spam in February 2004 hosted by the European Commission in Brussels.[2]

Spam is a cross-cutting issue impacting on network utilisation, congestion issues, and Internet issues; privacy and network security issues; and consumer protection issues. In order to better co-ordinate work on spam and assist in obtaining a more rapid consensus on a policy framework to tackle spam issues the OECD Council agreed in July 2004 to set up a horizontal "Task Force on Spam." The Task Force was requested to report to the CP and ICCP Committees by July 2006.

The primary objective of the Task Force was to bring together designated anti-spam policy co-ordinators and allow for the most effective preparation of urgently needed policy tools to combat spam, approaching the problem in a broader way and benefiting from the multi-disciplinary expertise of OECD.

The Task Force was asked to study, document and promote the range of existing and emerging anti-spam strategies across all sectors. Recognising that there is no "silver bullet" to tackle spam, the Task Force developed an Anti-Spam Toolkit ("the Toolkit"). The Toolkit is based on the premise that a number of co-ordinated different elements need to be brought to bear on the problem of spam to help the development and growth of anti-spam strategies and solutions in the technical, regulatory and enforcement fields and to facilitate international co-operation. The OECD Toolkit is aimed at bringing together a set of consistent and complementary policy and other (*e.g.* enforcement) initiatives. The elaboration and implementation of the Toolkit relied substantively on the input of stakeholders in the various areas covered. The Toolkit is composed of eight interrelated elements:

- Anti-spam regulation.
- International enforcement co-operation.
- Industry-driven solutions against spam.
- Existing and emerging anti-spam technologies.
- Education and awareness.
- Co-operative partnerships against spam.
- Spam metrics.
- Global co-operation (Outreach).

Background reports were prepared for the Task Force for several of the elements of the Toolkit.[3] This report synthesises the work which has been undertaken by the Task Force and its conclusions. The Report is complemented by the OECD Council Recommendation on Spam Cross-Border Enforcement Co-operation, and the OECD Anti-Spam Web site (www.oecd-antispam.org).

The work of the Task Force has already made an important contribution toward co-operative efforts to combat spam. The Task Force has focused international attention and resources at the issue of spam, and the concerted efforts of government, industry, and civil society have surely contributed to limiting this problem. The broad dissemination and implementation of the Toolkit can continue to have a positive impact in this area.

Status and evolution of spam

At the end of 2004 the total number of Internet users in the world reached 380 million. About 42% of them have broadband connections with "always on" capabilities.[4] Most of these users are in OECD countries, where broadband subscribers increased from 118 million at the end of 2004 to 137 million by mid-2005.[5] As ICT networks develop, however, besides the creation of an increasing range of opportunities, a host of new challenges arise.

In particular, as stressed in the "*OECD Guidelines for the Security of Information Systems and Networks: Towards a Culture of Security*", the reliability and efficiency of platforms, application and services, and the confidence of users in their utilisation, are fundamental elements in enabling the benefits ICT can bring to economic and social development.[6] However, today the reliability of e-mail and other electronic communication tools – and consequently users' trust and confidence in these technologies – is threatened by the escalation of unsolicited/unwanted electronic messages, commonly known as spam, which are flooding the Internet and causing significant harm to both individuals and businesses.

Spam, which began as messages advertising commercial products or services, grew exponentially, reaching its highest point in 2004. In addition, simple advertising messages have evolved into messages that are potentially dangerous, as opposed to merely annoying. Spam messages nowadays have a deceptive nature, may cause network disruptions, and are used as a vehicle for spreading viruses, thus undermining consumer confidence, which is a prerequisite for the information society and for the success of e-commerce. This evolution (see Figure 1) can be summarised looking at three main changes:

- Firstly, spammers implemented new technical and social methods to disguise the origin of their messages, thus eluding adverse action by law enforcement authorities, ISPs and individuals. These techniques include address spoofing, utilisation of open relays or open proxies, and increasingly robot networks ("botnets").

- Secondly, in the past months spam has grown into a vehicle for the diffusion of a host of threats, facilitating the spread of viruses and other malicious software (malware) and serving as the vehicle for fraud, such as phishing.[7]

- Thirdly, spam activities, once limited to e-mail, are now spreading to new communication technologies, including mobile devices – such as personal digital assistants (PDAs) and smart phones – which are increasingly used to access electronic mail messages. In addition spam has invaded instant messaging services, blogs, and threatens to taint voice over IP applications (see figure below).

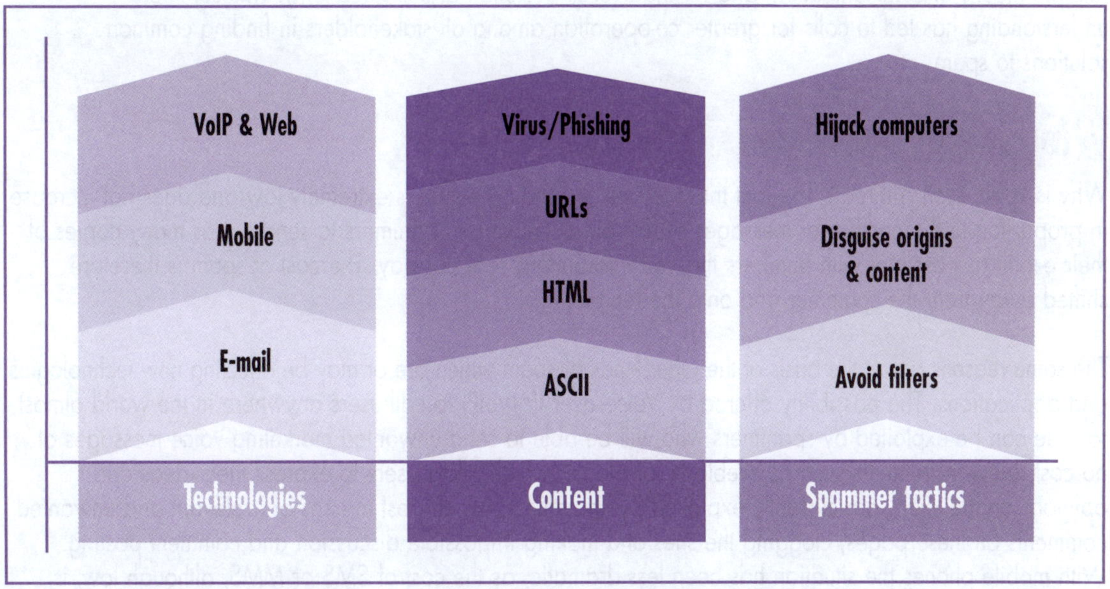

Figure 1. Spam evolution

There is no internationally agreed definition of spam, which is defined differently in national legislative approaches. For this reason the Task Force has not attempted to classify spam. Nevertheless, there are common characteristics that countries have recognised in their definitions:

- **Electronic message**: spam messages are sent electronically. While e-mail is by far the most significant channel for spam, other delivery channels are also considered in a number of countries (mobile spam, such as SMS and MMS, spam over IP, etc).

- **Hidden or false message origins**: spam messages are often sent in a manner that disguises the originator by using false header information. Spammers frequently use unauthorised third-party e-mail servers.

- Spam does not offer a **valid and functional address** to which recipients may send messages opting out of receiving further unsolicited messages.

- **Illegal or offensive content**: spam is frequently a vehicle for fraudulent or deceptive content, viruses, etc. Other spam includes adult or offensive content, which may be illegal in some countries, especially if it is sent to minors.

- **Utilization of addresses without the owner's consent**: Spammers often use e-mail addresses that have been collected without the owner's explicit consent. This is frequently done through software programmes which gather addresses from the Web or create e-mail addresses (harvesting and dictionary attacks).

- **Bulk and repetitive**: spam messages are typically sent in bulk in an indiscriminate manner, without any knowledge about the recipient other than the e-mail address.

In conclusion, there is a common understanding that spam is a threat to the Internet as an effective and reliable means of communication, and for the overall evolution of the e-economy. This common understanding has led to calls for greater co-operation among all stakeholders in finding common solutions to spam.

Why spam? How does it work?

Why is spam such a threat? The fact that the cost of sending e-mail is extremely low and does not increase in proportion to the number of messages sent is an incentive for spammers to send out as many copies of their e-mail as possible, with numbers that run into billions sent per day. The cost of spam is therefore shifted away from the spammer and onto the recipient.

The same reasons are at the basis of the other kinds of spam which are or may be affecting new technologies and applications. The possibility offered by Voice over IP (VoIP) to call users anywhere in the world almost for free can be exploited by spammers who will be able to send unwanted marketing voice messages at no cost. New instruments such as Weblogs (or blogs), which allow users to express their ideas and opinions on the Web, are currently exploited by spammers, which post masses of irrelevant and unwanted comments on these pages, clogging the sites and making impossible discussion and comment posting. With mobile phones the situation has been less dramatic, as the cost of SMS or MMS, although low, is preventing mass spamming. A short summary of the different kinds of spam and their effects is below.

E-mail spam

To understand why e-mail spam is such a problem, and how the possible solutions work, it is necessary to understand how Internet e-mail works. Basically, the Internet standard mechanism commonly used to relay e-mail messages is the Simple Mail Transfer Protocol, or SMTP. This protocol "submits" the message to the network, starting a "five-part dialogue", which takes place between the different involved computers. The computer that submits the message is referred to generally as the SMTP client.

In the SMTP standard, all e-mails have an envelope and a header.[8] The envelope information is meant for the hosts performing message transfer and is not usually seen by end users. Envelope information is exchanged during the SMTP protocol's five-part dialogue. In theory, at transmission-time, envelope information gets memorialised in "headers" that the recipient can view. Headers are the parts of the e-mail above the message body.

In its present state, there are two main types of vulnerability in the SMTP authentication process that spammers exploit.[9]

- No authentication is required, therefore users have the ability to hide their identity, as usually happens in spam cases.

- Every piece of information in an e-mail message (in the envelope that the human receiver does not see as well as in the header that the human receiver may see) can be forged.

One of the consequences of these SMTP vulnerability attacks is e-mail spoofing, *i.e.* when the headers and/or e-mail content is forged. When this happens, the recipient of the falsified e-mail can be misled by what they read, thinking the e-mail is about something it's not and/or that the e-mail came from someone they trust (See also Paragraph on "phishing" below).

In addition, the financial burden of sending the message is imposed on the network and the recipient.

Mobile spam

Mobile spam is a term typically used to refer to unsolicited communications sent via SMS or MMS. To date, mobile spam usually consists in:

- SMS or MMS advertising a commercial service or product.

- SMS or MMS soliciting a premium or international rate response from the recipient. These kinds of messages are typically deceptive or fraudulent, and are also known as "scam" messages.

It is important to note that while with the advent of third generation services it is now common to receive e-mails on mobile devices, there is a difference between mobile specific services – such as communications sent via SMS, which are sent and received within the mobile environment – and other services, such as e-mail, which are not mobile-specific, but emerge from the Internet environment and are a result of fixed/mobile convergence.

Whilst Internet e-mail spam has become a major issue for customers, mobile spam, to date, has not been a problem in the same order of magnitude. This is predominantly due to the commercial and service environment for mobile-specific services, which is inherently more resistant to spam. Examples of factors and measures that contribute to this environment include:

- Economic measures: "Calling party pays" principles, withholding of fraudulent premium service payments, revision of roaming agreements to cover SMS and MMS.

- Customer tools: spam reporting facilities, unsubscribe mechanisms.

- Technical initiatives: network filtering or traffic analysis to identify unusual activity commonly associated with mobile spam, where the legislation allows them.

In most countries there are national laws relevant to unsolicited SMS and MMS, and mobile operators usually have procedures for identifying and dealing with fraudulent messaging. Those also include, in addition to the measures listed above, co-operation activities with relevant public authorities. However, where mobile spam is sent across networks or at the international level, it can be harder to combat. Industry associations, such as the GSM Association (GSMA)[10], developed information and recommended procedures to help mobile operators work together in order to identify and address these problems, and set up international working groups on mobile spam, which facilitate international co-operation and exchange of best practices among operators. The development of a Mobile Spam Code of Practice is also planned.

Voice over IP spam (SPIT) and spam over multimedia IP applications

Spam is not limited to e-mails, but is spreading to other emerging technologies such as VoIP. Some of the problems which have been identified up to now include those usually associated with IP networks, plus other more sophisticated threats, such as misrepresentation, eavesdropping, VoIP specific Denial of Service attacks,[11] packet injections and unwanted messages (spam over VoIP, or SPIT). The latter is mainly due to the possibility offered by VoIP of sending voice messages at a very low cost, which may lead to a situation similar to the one already experienced with e-mail spam: large amounts of unwanted voicemail messages can be sent through the world in a few seconds, and cause problems similar to those mentioned in the introduction.

Voice over IP is only the first of a long series of new applications and services which will be available with the advent of Next Generation Networks. New multimedia services, based on SIP[12] and IMS[13], for example, are being developed, and will allow mobile instant messaging, push-to-talk-over-cellular, video-sharing, and multiplayer-games in the future. Once again, however, the security aspect needs to be addressed, in order to protect IP multimedia applications from new kinds of spam and, in general, from security threats.

Search Engine spam

In the rapidly expanding Internet world, where there are an estimated 83 million registered domain names and 75 million Web sites[14], it is becoming increasingly common for users to utilise search engines in order to find Web pages and content that is more relevant to them.

However, as happened in the case of e-mails, new services and applications quickly become new opportunities for fraud. Search engine spam exploits the search mechanism to push a specific Web page (pornographic sites, Viagra, financial, etc.) to the top of search rankings. There are different possible methods used to reach this objective, which can be more or less sophisticated. "Search spam" consists in machine-generated pages designed to appear in the engines to attract traffic (and ultimately increase revenue); in other cases Webmasters hide non-visible links to advertiser sites on their Web page in order to drive up advertisers' PageRank without that being apparent to anyone.[15]

Blog spam and Splogs

Another method used by spammers to advertise their Web sites is "link spam" or "blog comment spam", in which automated bots attach advertisement links on the comments pages of blogs. In certain cases splogs – a combination of spam and blogs – are created using automated programmes that randomly compose them using catchwords scoring well in search engines. In October 2005 the blog hosting service "Blogger" faced an avalanche of 13 000 splogs created in a single week. Search engines such as Google and Yahoo! are trying to improve their parameters in order to exclude this kind of pages from their results.[16]

The rise of this phenomenon is damaging the functionality of blogs, and increasing the problem of reliability of information on the Internet. Blogs – a revolutionary instruments allowing all users to express and confront their ideas on the Web – risk today being clogged with spam comments, ultimately impeding the utilisation of the site.

Spam and phishing

"Phishing" is the name attributed to online identity theft perpetrated through the sending of e-mail messages falsely claiming to be from established and legitimate companies that try to trick users into disclosing their personal information, such as credit card numbers or passwords. Frequently these messages, or the Web sites that they link to, try to install malicious code.[17]

The term was well chosen by computer experts in the late 90s, when the phenomenon appeared for the first time: in phishing the phisher uses the e-mail message as a bait to lure users – in the Internet sea – to disclose information.

The vector used for phishing attacks are spam e-mails sent out to millions of users. In the past few years, phishing attacks have been growing in number and sophistication,[18] so that messages are carefully crafted to impersonate known, trustworthy financial institutions or organisations. Phishers use spam techniques to make their e-mails appear to be from the targeted companies; they can easily copy logos and information present in the company's Web site and use corporate text and graphics.[19] Phishing messages are also tailored to users in different countries, featuring local language and names of national banks and operators.

In order to avoid detection, phishing attacks are transient and short-lived, usually occurring only for a very short time span before disappearing.[20] For the same reason phishers need to act very dynamically. Phishers typically exploit software vulnerabilities in servers and their operating systems in order to install their content, and need to move quickly and easily between servers to confuse the true source of the attack or in case a compromised site is discovered and taken offline.

The information obtained by phishers is used to access bank accounts and withdraw money, or to open new bank or credit card accounts in the victim's name, causing major financial disruptions to those involved. Recently phishing techniques have been used for industrial espionage and for the extortion of sensitive data (see Box 1).

Box 1. Spear-phishing

A new form of phishing, known as "spear-phishing" has emerged in the past months, raising alarm in the Internet community. In "Spear-phishing" scammers send messages to people within a small group – for example a company or government offices – instead of to millions of e-mail users. Targets are carefully selected: false e-mail messages are personalized and specifically directed to users who have an established relationship with the sender being impersonated, making attacks more difficult to detect and neutralise. Spear-phishing is a sort of social engineering – the practice of obtaining confidential information by manipulation of legitimate users – which is used, among the others, for corporate espionage, as the recipient reveals information and passwords that will enable the criminal to access secure areas of the corporate network, which can result in the theft of intellectual property and other sensitive corporate documents and data.[21]

How much does spam cost?

Internet users incur a direct cost resulting from the time spent consulting, identifying and deleting unwanted messages. In addition, they are concerned about the reliability of communications and the content of spam messages. The new possibilities offered by broadband "always-on", fast Internet connections are hampered by dangers linked to spam: deceptive or misleading messages, offensive content, goods and services of a dubious nature offered for sale.

For professional and business users, spam represents a loss of productivity, and imposes direct costs by increasing the need for technical support and software solutions such as filters. Spam imposes more general societal costs by reducing the reliability of e-mail as a communication tool (legitimate messages can be blocked by filters or be lost among a large number of unsolicited e-mails), and threatening the security of a company's internal network.

The other major victims of spam are ISPs and other network operators, which process e-mails. Increased costs derive from the need to implement anti-spam solutions, such as filters, the increased necessity of technical support, costs associated with expanding infrastructure to handle the amount of messages, and the risk – in cases where ISPs are used by spammers, or computers in their networks are hijacked – to lose reputation or even to be blocked by other ISPs. Many of these costs will subsequently be passed on to the consumer in the form of higher access fees or poorer service.

The actual cost of spam is difficult to calculate, as some of the damages are only indirect, and whether and how to cost the time of private individuals is controversial. In addition, the fraudulent nature of spam, or the malware carried by spam messages, can result in more important financial damages to users and companies (see for example the paragraphs on spam and phishing).

Unwanted messages are creating problems and additional costs to users not only in OECD countries, but also in developing and least developed economies. The latter have a less extendsive Internet infrastructure, and often have relatively less available bandwidth. Individuals in developing economies often access Internet through dial-up connections, or from community access points, such as cybercafés, where the user pays on the basis of the time spent onl ine. Under these conditions it is easy to see how spam takes up a valuable part of the already limited resources, increases the cost of Internet access, and reduces the quality of service.[22]

The following sections provide an overview of the work of the Task Force for each of the elements of the anti-spam Toolkit.

ELEMENT I – ANTI-SPAM REGULATION

Broad considerations for spam regulation

In the past few years several countries – mostly those in the OECD area – have been developing and implementing specific legislation to deal with the growing problem of spam. The work by the Task Force on anti-spam regulatory approaches highlights the main elements which could be considered by countries in view of implementing effective legislation. This element's work is based on the Task Force "Anti-Spam Regulation" Report.[23]

Spam is a "horizontal" issue, touching upon different aspects of telecommunication services, consumer protection, security, and privacy, at national and cross-border levels. Accordingly, the legal framework that has been put in place is complex, owing in particular to the several national public and private enforcement agencies that are dealing with this topic and the need to cover different types of spam.

Before beginning this section, it is worth noting that as the legal, political and cultural environments of different countries vary, there is not a global uniform approach to spam or a common definition of spam accepted at the international level. For this reason the Toolkit, rather than advocate a single approach, aims to underline decision points that need to be discussed while elaborating anti-spam legislation and examine the related policy questions.[24] In this report the term spam refers to electronic messages that are defined to be illegal in their national legislation.

Measures taken to prevent spam are designed to meet a number of policy goals and objectives:

- **To preserve the benefits of electronic communications** by increasing the trust of users in the messaging media and improving the availability, reliability and cost of the service. The level of spam has now reached the point where it is impacting on users' confidence in using e-mail and other messaging media, and having a negative impact on the performance of global communication networks.

- **To prohibit and apply sanctions against the act of spamming, as defined by national law**. Legislation alone will not stop potential spammers from taking advantage of this marketing technique; however laws and regulations can have an impact as they apply sanctions against those individuals and organizations that choose to make use of spam. The value of the legislation, however, will depend on the gravity of sanctions, and on the certainty of their application.

- **To reduce the amount of spam**. Activities need to be targeted at different stages, to prevent spam from being sent, reduce the volume of spam traversing networks, and reduce the amount of spam received by end-users. Examples of provisions relating to these three objectives may include: *i*) forbid harvesting techniques and software; encourage implementation of Acceptable Use Policy by ISPs, *ii*) allow ISPs to block users sending spam, *iii*) promote utilisation of filters.

In pursuing these goals, the legislator should take into consideration four general principles:

- **Policy direction**: The legislation should provide a clear policy direction. The main lines and objectives of the national anti-spam policy should be drawn at an earlier stage and need to underlie the entire governmental strategy (including enforcement and educational initiatives, for example).

- **Regulatory simplicity**: The legislation should be short and simple.

- **Enforcement effectiveness**: Enforcement is a fundamental issue, which, if not dealt with appropriately, can make a good piece of legislation useless. For this reason it is important to put in place an effective sanction regime and appropriate standards of proof. In addition, effective powers and resources need to be provided for enforcement authorities (see Element II).

- **International linkages**: As spam is an international issue, the legislation should enable appropriate international linkages, and provide national authorities with the possibility to co-operate in investigations and exchange information with foreign authorities (see Element II).

Anti-spam checklist

To design a regulatory approach that appropriately targets the anti-spam policy goals and principles identified above, a series of questions need to be answered:

✓ Nature of spam and objectives of the legislation?

✓ Technical element: technology-by-technology description or technology neutral approach?

✓ Consent: express, inferred, assumed? Who bears the burden of proof?

- ✓ Commercial element: marketing purposes / financial gain? Only commercial messages should be targeted?
- ✓ Sender information: which information should be included in a message?
- ✓ Bulk – how 'bulk' should be defined?
- ✓ Privacy considerations: spam and abuse of personal data (e-mail addresses, etc.).
- ✓ Content: Do existing laws deal adequately with misleading and fraudulent content?
- ✓ Ancillary elements: should regulatory response also cover activities ancillary to the sending of spam?
- ✓ Additional requirements: address harvesting, dictionary attacks, labelling?

The considerations that should be taken into account in answering these questions will be dealt with in more detail in the next section.

Anti-spam regulatory approach: elements

Services concerned

Services concerned → Technical element: technology-by-technology description or technology neutral approach?	• Electronic message: focuses on a specific messaging medium (e-mail), or does it include "electronic messages" in general, such as IM, SMS, MMS, mobile e-mails and spam over VoIP?

The legislative definition of spam may focus on a particular messaging medium, or attempt to provide a technology neutral approach that provides an overarching statement of principles that is more broadly applicable.

Restricting the scope of the legislation means that it may be necessary to update laws regularly to face new threats and cover new emerging technologies and applications. However, even with a technology neutral approach, it is worthwhile to evaluate which particular messaging media are being misused or have a strong potential to be misused in the future and ensure that they are appropriately addressed in the legislation.

One reason behind this legislative approach is to cover all communication media which have a marginal cost near to zero for the sender, while imposing a disproportionate burden (financial, time loss, etc.) on the recipient and on the network in general.[25]

Although the most urgent problem for many countries is e-mail spam, countries with a strong take-up of third generation mobile telephony have found that SMS and MMS spam is of increasing concern. In some jurisdictions new means of communications are being exploited by spammers, who are expanding their scope using a range of new messaging opportunities such as wikis,[26] blogs, and short range wireless communications (Bluetooth/wireless network devices).

In developing an anti-spam regulatory approach the policy maker should consider that with the convergence of messaging format, allowed by the emergence of new technologies and applications, such as 3G and 4G or Voice over IP (VoIP), new and unforeseen messaging media may arise. New legislation should therefore be sufficiently flexible to ensure that communication technologies are covered in the event that they are subject to new forms of spam. At the same time it should be recognized that any policy or regulatory regime imposed on a messaging technology is going to have an impact on legitimate messaging, as well as the spam messages being targeted.

Nature of the message

Commercial purpose → Nature of spam and objectives of the legislation?	• Consider whether legislation should only address commercial and transactional messages, or whether it should also address specific non-commercial content, such as political or religious messages.

A large percentage of spam is aimed at making money through the sale of goods or services or through some sort of fraud. For this reason, many legislative definitions of spam stress the commercial nature of the messages. While a focus on commercial messages would clarify that personal, political, religious or ideological messages would not be restricted by anti-spam activities, and that therefore the regulatory efforts against spam will not have negative impacts on freedom of speech or expression, it should be noted that not all spam is of a commercial nature. Limiting the scope of spam legislation to commercial messages only may lead to the omission of most harmful spam. For example, a million spam messages promoting a political or religious idea can be as invasive and disturbing as a million messages promoting a herbal remedy.

In the United States the CAN-SPAM Act covers only commercial e-mail. It defines as commercial any electronic mail message of which the primary purpose is the commercial advertisement or promotion of a commercial product or service. The EU Electronic Communications Privacy Directive covers principally messages sent "for the purposes of direct marketing", while Australia, after defining commercial electronic message specifies that the sending of certain kind of messages – such as for example messages sent by government bodies, religious organizations, or by academic institutions to their alumni – is not subject to the limitations foreseen by Section 16 of the Act ("unsolicited commercial electronic messages must not be sent").

Consent

A fundamental principle involved in many anti-spam regulatory arrangements is that e-mails of a commercial nature can only be sent to individuals or organisations where they have consented to receive such material. A number of conceptual frameworks have been utilised in relation to consent, including opt-in and opt-out models – depending on whether an activity is based on the permission of the recipient (ergo the term "permission-based marketing") prior to receiving the electronic message – 'opt-in' – or after receiving it – 'opt-out' – and provisions that allow for consent to be inferred where there is a pre-existing relationship.

As well as being explicitly identified and legislated for, the concept of consent can also be incorporated through the application of personal and data privacy regimes, which may include a presumption that unless consent has been given, then a person may not be approached or specific information (such as an e-mail address) traded or exchanged. The essential issue is the degree of consent or permission which legislators or regulators wish to require in specified circumstances.

Public debate about consent has tended to focus on the issue of 'opt-in' provisions versus 'opt-out'. While this debate was appropriate in the past, it is becoming less useful over time as many recent approaches to spam regulation have incorporated more complex or subtle methods involving express consent, inferred consent, implied consent, assumed consent or a blend of these.[27] These concepts are explored in more detail below. It is important to remember that consent is often only one element of a spam definition or approach. Most of the spam received by users is in fact violating more than one legal provision, as they have hidden or falsified header information, they do not provide any unsubscribe address, and often contain misleading proposals or carry viruses.

Consent: express, inferred, assumed? Who bears the burden of proof?	Description	Pro	Cons
Express consent	Form of consent where an individual or organisation has actively given their consent to a particular action or activity.	– Protect users privacy, providing more control on personal data. – It can result in a much higher response rate for legitimate online marketers as the messages are from from known or trusted senders, and therefore are much more likely to be read and relevant to the recipient. – The burden of proving that consent has been given lies with the sender of the message, not with the recipient.	– Difficulty in keeping records of received consent by business. The absence of such records may significantly restrict the potential pool of recipients who can be targeted for otherwise legitimate messaging. – Restricts "commercial free speech" – Could result in devoting enforcement resources in areas where consumers are not financially harmed.
Inferred and implicit consent	This is consent which generally can be inferred from the conduct and/or other business relationships of the recipient.	– More flexible.	– It may be difficult to define when a message can be related to an existent "business relationship".
Assumed consent	There is a presumption of consent until it is removed by the recipient, for example by "unsubscribing" or by placing their electronic address on a do-not-contact-list.	– Less constrictive to the operation of online commerce; minimal risk of inadvertently proscribing legitimate messaging. – Does not restrict choice of e-mail recipients who want to receive commercial messages.	– It transfers the burden of effort and cost to the consumer. – In order to unsubscribe the e-mail must be opened and responded to, which is contrary to good e-security practice, unless the e-mail is from a known and trusted source. – Unsubscribe links are often non-functional. – It places the evidentiary burden upon the recipient of the message.
Blended approaches to consent	Some recent approaches to anti-spam legislation have provided a "blended" or situational approach to consent.		

Whether the sender did or did not have the consent of the recipient for sending the message would be useful in limiting cases of aggressive direct marketing practices, by targeting companies that are either unaware of, or ignore, anti spam legislation, and helping to protect consumers from unsolicited advertising that–with the advent of new technologies – can become particularly intrusive. In addition, with opt-in rules the burden of proof is on the sender, who will have to demonstrate that he/she obtained the prior consent of the recipient, or had a prior commercial relationship with the subject. In the case where the sender is a legitimate marketer violating only opt-in requirements, it will be easier for the public or private enforcement agency to intervene, as the sender is known, easy to contact, and usually respects the law. Actions should be prioritised, to devote resources to enforcement against the most harmful types of spam.

Removing consent or "Unsubscribing"

Unsubscribe address	
→ The recipient of electronic messages should always be able to unsubscribe from the mailing list, requesting that such communication cease.	• Almost all legislation currently implemented foresees that a **valid return address** (or number) should be included in messages, so that the recipient may easily unsubscribe, without any additional cost. In some cases a postal address should also be provided. • The sender is given a period of time (for example 10 days) to comply and cease the transmission. • Any transmission of messages after the recipient opted-out is not permitted.

The ability of a recipient to remove consent, often through some form of "unsubscribe facility", is generally fundamental in spam legislation as users and consumers may not be, or are no longer, interested in receiving messages from a certain sender. In order to unsubscribe it would be necessary that the sender provides an opt-out address, which the recipient will be able to contact at no cost. In addition, the law should establish a time period for the sender to comply with the request. Any message sent after that date will be considered as spam.

The Australian legislation states that any commercial electronic message has to contain functional unsubscribe facilities, *i.e.* an address that the recipient may use to send an unsubscribe message. These facilities have to be easily and readily available for users. Similar provisions are included in the EU directive and the U.S. CAN SPAM Act.

This provision is meant to give the user the possibility to stop the receipt of messages; however its concrete application presents several problems, most notably in case the opt-out address is false, or the opt-out option is not respected by the sender. In the latter situation the recipient, replying to spam mail, may simply confirm that his/her address is active, potentially provoking an even higher flux of spam messages to their inbox. For this reason, while appropriate legislation and effective enforcement are essential, governments should also raise awareness among consumers of the possible risks one can incur with e-mail, and educate users on how to recognize a spam e-mail and deal with it.

Information about message origins

Header information and sender ID	
→ A key challenge in the regulation of spamming activities, and the enforcement of spam laws, is the ability of spammers to obfuscate the origin of spam being sent.	• Legislation needs to **prohibit the sending of e-mails with falsified origins or concealed header/ID information**. • Legislation should also require that the marketer supporting the sender should be **clearly identified**.

One of the main problems with the e-mail system is that e-mail was never designed to be secure, but mainly to be functional and easy to use.[28] Today, these characteristics, which have made it so successful, are at the root of the problem. Spammers can send thousands of messages at little cost, and at the same time can hide or falsify their identity information. For this reason the prohibition to send commercial electronic messages disguising or concealing identity information is included in all the anti-spam legislative instruments currently implemented.

This requirement is thought to be essential in combating the use of spam to spread scams, frauds, or viruses. At the same time, however, it is one of the most difficult provisions to enforce, as once the sender has disguised or falsified the header information, it will be very difficult for an enforcement agency to identify them, and investigations are usually complex, expensive and time consuming. In this context, it is important to ensure that enforcement bodies possess technical expertise, and that physical and financial evidence should be admitted for the enforcement of anti-spam laws or in taking action against spammers. In addition, technical instruments should be developed to support the legislative effort; the development and implementation of e-mail authentication solutions[29] is currently being studied and its merits and shortcomings will be analysed more in detail in the section dealing with "technical measures".

Ancillary elements

It is easy to consider spam as an activity only undertaken by the person who hits the "send" button. It can, however, be considered more broadly – often spam is sent on behalf of a third party, who hope to sell goods or services to people responding to the messages. Increasingly, spam campaigns are being set up so that the person (or a Trojan-controlled computer) sending the message is several steps removed from the person that actually decided that the message should be sent and who may profit from responses to spam. There is potential for a regulatory response to target the people who decide to send spam, or who collaborate in its sending, as well as the person physically responsible for sending it. There are a number of activities that serve to enable people to undertake spam campaigns. These include:

- The utilisation of software that harvests contact details and e-mail addresses from the Internet.
- The sale of address lists.
- The operation of "spammer friendly" ISPs.

It is important to note that there are beneficial and legitimate uses of address harvesting software (Webmasters could run the software against their own site, for instance, as a way of checking what contact addresses were being made publicly available). A regulatory strategy in respect of address harvesting, sale of lists or provision of a "safe harbour" ISP should only address these activities insofar as they relate to the sending of spam.

Harvesting software and harvested address lists: Address harvesting software collects people's contact details without their knowledge or permission. **Dictionary attacks**: Addresses are automatically generated based on words from a dictionary, common names and numbers.	Legislation may include specific provisions to levy additional sanctions if such tools are used to aid the sending of spam in contravention of the jurisdiction's spam legislation.

Sanctions should be applied not only against the person materially sending the spam, but also to those commissioning, authorizing this activity or otherwise benefiting from spam activity, and who normally share the profits resulting from spam.

Person authorizing the sending of the spam or aiding/assisting the spammer	The law should address the person physically sending the message, and also the person who commissioned or authorised the messages to be sent or who have gained financially through spamming activities.

Besides targeting an additional wrongdoer, this approach could facilitate enforcement, as it is often difficult to determine who actually sent the spam while it may be easier to determine the marketer benefiting from spamming activity. This possibility therefore presents two major advantages:

- First, money and goods are physical assets and their transfer can be followed more easily.
- Second, it is more likely that the seller/advertiser has more assets that can be used to pay damages to recipients of spam.

Cybercrime and content-related questions

Although spam in itself constitutes an abuse, recently there has been a shift toward the inclusion in spam messages of content that is increasingly malicious. Cybercrimes are committed to improve spamming techniques – for example using Trojan software and hijacked computers – and in turn spamming techniques are used to perpetrate crimes on line (the case of online frauds, phishing, etc) and to spread security threats – such as in the case of viruses and spyware. As with other content-related issues associated with spam, the decision as to whether this should be addressed by the anti-spam regulatory regime is best decided with reference to the national circumstances. It should be recognised, however, that in many countries this malware aspect of spam is criminalised by statute or can be readily criminalised using the Council of Europe Convention on Cybercrime framework.

Illegal access

Misuse of computer resources	
→ Spammers are increasingly using botnets, or zombie computers to send their messages, to disguise the origin of the spam, and to have a greater amount of network and processing capacity at their disposal.	Legislation **should forbid the unauthorized use of protected computer resources**. Anybody compromising computers and using these to send messages should be sanctioned.

One of the developments in the spam area which is raising concerns among users and providers, is the techniques spammers are using to send messages by exploiting computer and network resources belonging to third parties. These systems use open relays, and more recently botnets or zombie computers, *i.e.* machines that have been compromised through the use of Trojans[30] and can be remotely controlled, to send spam hiding its origin and making it virtually impossible to trace the spammer.

The Council of Europe Convention on Cybercrime foresees in art. 2 that *"the access to the whole or any part of a computer system without right"* has to be considered a criminal offence. This provision has been implemented in several countries.[31]

Misleading or fraudulent content

Spam has evolved from an annoying marketing method into a vehicle for scams, misleading trade practices, offensive content and dangerous viruses, increasing the costs and the risks to users.

Misleading or fraudulent content → Content of dubious nature. Many spam messages are today a vehicle for fraud (as for example phishing scams).	– Spam scams and phishing could constitute computer-related offences, i.e. ordinary crimes that are frequently committed through the use of a computer system. – Spam legislation may cover the content of the message, in particular in case anti-fraud laws, consumer protection legislation, etc. are not clearly drawn out. – The prohibition of misleading or deceptive subject headings is contained in some legislation.
Security threats → Spam is increasingly used to distribute viruses, worms and spyware: as in the case above, the focus is on the message content.	– Malware aspects of spam are often criminalised by statute or can be criminalised using the Council of Europe Convention on Cybercrime framework.

The focus in these cases shifts from the vehicle (the spam), to its content (*e.g.* fraud, virus). Many aspects are already covered by national anti-fraud laws, or criminal provisions. While some countries prefer to maintain general, technology-neutral anti-fraud and criminal laws, others may want to consider revamping these norms to respond to new Internet threats.[32]

At the international level one of the leading efforts was undertaken by the Council of Europe with the Convention on Cybercrime.[33] The Convention tries to provide a comprehensive instrument to deal with cybercrime in a more harmonised and co-ordinated manner. In addition, the Convention supports the adoption at the national level of criminal laws prohibiting:

The access to the whole or any part of a computer system without right (see above, computer misuse).

- Interception without right, made by technical means, of non-public transmissions of computer data to, from or within a computer system.
- Damaging, deletion, deterioration, alteration or suppression of computer data without right.
- Computer-related fraud.
- Offences related to child pornography.

Bulk

Bulk	
→ Bulk should be characterised as an element of spam? How should it be defined? How will standard spammer techniques of avoiding bulk provisions be dealt with?	• Legislation may foresee that e-mail is classified as spam only if a certain number of messages have been sent in a given period of time (usually over 50-100 over 24 hours) • This element of course needs to be considered with the others as not all bulk e-mail is spam (e.g. newsletters, etc)

An option available to spam regulators is to specify a quantum of e-mails, whereby e-mails sent above this cut-off point are designated as spam and therefore prohibited. This has generally been set at the level of 50 to 100 e-mails.[34] However, such an approach is not without problems, as it is arbitrary in nature, as not all bulk e-mail is spam, and simple technical arrangements and legal arguments can be employed in order to prevent messages from being classified as "bulk" (for example sending multiple flights of messages, or using multiple addresses to send the messages).

A person who receives an unsolicited commercial message will generally not care, nor be able to discover, if the message has been sent to them singly, or to a million other recipients. In most countries a single electronic message can still be defined as spam, if it violates the national anti-spam legislation, and it will be up to the recipient, or the enforcement agency, to decide whether to take action against the sender or not on a case-by-case basis, depending on the gravity of the violation and the available resources.

Labelling

Labelling	
→ Labelling e-mail involves the inclusion of a short name (as for example [adv] for advertising) to identify the content of a particular e-mail. This simplifies filtering, in particular to block e-mails containing pornographic material sent to children.	• Legislation could include a provision requiring the use of a specific label for e-mail containing advertising, pornographic material, etc.

The utilization of specific wording, or labels, to allow users to distinguish between advertising and other personal and professional e-mail, could be useful in the fight against spam. In terms of e-mail, labelling is the use of standard words in the message header or subject line that clearly identifies the content of the message, for example, the use of "ADV" for advertising and "ADLT" for adult content. Such a mechanism means that recipients are able to distinguish between advertising material and other e-mail traffic. It would also enable the more efficient and effective use of filtering systems.

There are several limitations in relation to this approach:

- Variations on labelling, may result in the evasion of filtering systems, for example, "A.D.V." or "a d v" instead of "ADV".
- Labelling would mostly be an effective anti-spam tool only if an internationally harmonised approach were adopted.
- Spam offenders, especially those that obscure their identity and do not provide accurate contact details, are unlikely to comply with such a requirement.

Cross-border issues

Cross-border jurisdiction	
→ It is difficult to impose legislation on spam messages that have originated outside the jurisdiction of the recipient's country. At the same time, countries do not always have legal jurisdiction over spam messages that originate within their borders but are sent to a different country.	Regulation should create a link with domestic corporations and persons: • Limited provisions specifying that messages sent to or from the jurisdiction are covered, as well as messages commissioned from within the jurisdiction and financial benefits linked with spam (see example below). • Spammers who operate from national jurisdiction, even though they spam other countries, are effectively dealt with. • International co-operation and cross-border enforcement arrangements.

One of the major problems encountered by enforcement agencies in their fight against spammers is the difficulty to impose domestic legislation on spammers operating from outside the jurisdiction of the victim, and, vice-versa, some entities may have limited powers to intervene in the case of a spammer operating from their country who is only damaging users in a foreign territory. Also, in many instances one part of the evidence for a case is in another country, as happens for example in the case of investigations regarding banks accounts, intermediary companies, hosting companies, etc.

Extra-territorial jurisdiction, that is the legal authority of a government to exercise authority beyond its normal boundaries, is a potentially complex legal issue which may, as a matter of general legal policy, vary from country to country. However, it is increasingly common for countries to assert some form of extra-territorial jurisdiction in important legislation when appropriate.[35] For the purposes of preparing and implementing anti-spam regulation, the issues to consider are the necessity to incorporate measures that can practically be enforced by national courts; allow international agreements on the subject, and facilitate cross-border enforcement at the operational level (information exchange, co-operation in investigations). This issue will be discussed more in detail in the following section (Enforcement).

Identifying involved parties

As spam is a complex issue, a large number of parties are involved, such as users, ISPs, and enforcement agencies. Each of the players has different rights and responsibilities, which need to be addressed by the legislation.

Victims of spam are often **individual users** and consumers, whose rights need to be protected by appropriate legislation and the possibility of recourse. This involves, for example, setting-up ways for consumers to report spam violations to the enforcement agencies, or the creation of a transparent and time-effective claims procedures. Where a large number of individuals are receiving spam, the potential exists for classes of individuals to join together and launch class actions against spammers.[36] In such cases, challenges may be faced in terms of administrative issues, including the identification of individuals affected by a specific spam campaign, and the collection, retention and presentation of evidence. These issues, and the nature of spam being such that large numbers of parties may be sent spam, act against the likelihood of such a course of action.

Internet Service Providers have multiple roles when it comes to spam issues. They are victims of spam, which is clogging their networks and servers, and wasting storage resources, but they are also both a source of spam and the intermediary through which spam passes. With regard to this latter role of ISPs, it is essential that an anti-spam legislative/regulatory framework does not impose upon ISPs a sanction for merely being the conduit by which spam is distributed. The delivery of a message should not *per se* equate to a responsibility for its content, nor for the damage caused by its sending.

ISPs are also potentially an important repository of evidentiary material that can be critical in the enforcement of anti-spam laws. However, the nature of this role should be clearly articulated: it may be necessary/desirable to describe the role of ISPs in legislative terms. This could allow ISPs, for example, to avoid breaching privacy roles where they are acting in support of enforcement agencies. The use of Acceptable Use Policies (AUPs) by ISPs is another method by which the rights and responsibilities of ISPs can be described. An appropriately framed AUP can, in effect, allow ISPs to attain the status of self-nominated enforcer of anti-spam policies and make them a critical partner in the fight against spam.

Codes of conduct can also be developed by the ISPs and other online operators, such as direct marketers. Government and regulators can facilitate and support the development of codes that complement and are consistent with legislation (see Element III).

In anti-spam legislation, for example, it can be foreseen that bodies and associations in the communication sector develop industry codes relating to their activities. Guidance about the content of these codes can also be included in the legislation, which should however be limited to general lines and should not impose specific processes or solutions. In the case of codes of conduct for ISPs and online operators regarding unsolicited commercial messages, national law could encourage[37] industry to develop voluntary codes of practice and technical standards where they are in the public interest and do not impose undue financial and administrative burdens on industry participants. The law can foresee that the code would provide, for example:[38]

- The procedures to be followed by Internet service providers and electronic messaging service providers in dealing with unsolicited commercial electronic messages (including procedures relating to the use or provision of updated software for spam filtering).

- Information to users about dangers linked to spam, available technological solutions, utilisation of filters, etc.

- A list of actions to be taken in order to minimise or prevent the sending or delivery of unsolicited commercial electronic messages, including the correct configuration of servers so as to minimise or prevent the sending or delivery of spam, shutting down open relays, etc.

In the framework of the OECD Task Force activities a set of best practices for ISPs and network operators was developed by BIAC and the MAAWG (See Element III – Industry-driven initiatives). Similarly, note should also be taken of the GSMA code of practice (see Annex IV).

Legislation could also provide a comprehensive framework to support the activities of ISPs to block or limit the circulation of spam e-mail. One example is the Korean legislation, which legally grants ISPs the authorization to develop the criteria for blocking spam and develop means to prevent its circulation. Following the Korean text, when spam causes, or is expected to cause an unacceptable interruption of their services, or if a client does not want to receive spam, ISPs may reject the transmission of the spam in question. Similar results could be achieved through appropriate contractual provisions between ISPs and users.

Subjects involved	Role and needs
Individuals (natural persons)	Victims of spam, they need protection and recourse Possibility of class actions? Statutory damages?
Companies (legal persons)	Definition of their rights Consent (in case of opt-in): through authorised representative
Internet Service Providers	Damaged party – possibility of recourse? Repository of evidence. Enforcer of AUPs. Responsibility?
Telecom providers	(same as ISPs)
Government agencies	At national level there should be a public or private agency responsible for the enforcement of anti-spam legislation (such as, for example, the consumer protection agency, or the privacy protection authority). In case of spam constituting a criminal violation, law enforcement authorities are also involved. Co-operation between governmental agencies and criminal authorities should be encouraged
Other interests groups:	
Direct Marketing Associations	DMA code of practice.
Consumer protection associations	Education and awareness, enforcement.
Software providers	Responsibility of providers of CRM and harvesting tools – it could be inserted in the legislation as an ancillary element.

In setting the appropriate legislative framework, it needs to be considered how the legislation will be implemented and can practically be enforced by national courts and which provisions can be included to facilitate cross-border enforcement at the operational level. These issues will be the subject of the next section.

ELEMENT II – ANTI-SPAM ENFORCEMENT

Introduction

A survey by the OECD Task Force on Spam at the end of 2004 indicated that most OECD countries have, in the past few years, set up a legislative framework in order to fight spam.[39] European countries implemented Directive 58/2002 in which article 13 specifically addresses the problem of unsolicited electronic communications;[40] in Australia the Spam Act 2003 has been considered an example of good legislation for its inclusiveness;[41] Korea and the United States implemented their legislation respectively in 2001 and in 2003, adopting an opt-out approach,[42] in countries such as Canada, although there is no specific anti-spam legislation in place, laws protecting data privacy and consumer's rights are applied also to electronic messages, and messages violating these norms are considered as spam.[43] A Task Force in Canada recommended to the Minister of Industry that further legislative steps are required. A few countries are still in the process of creating anti-spam laws: New Zealand[44], for example, issued a discussion paper in 2004, and is in the process of approving legislation expected for 2006.[45]

While having the appropriate legislation is indeed necessary, the implementation and application of the law is a critical point, and constitutes the second step towards an inclusive anti-spam strategy. The timeliness and speed with which enforcement happens and sanctions are applied is crucial, if spam is to be effectively curbed: today spammers can move very fast and, if needed, relocate their entire operations within days if not hours. Traditional enforcement notices which can take several weeks or months are no more effective in the online world.

Governments, in furthering their work to facilitate anti-spam law enforcement across borders, may need to intervene in four main fields: national co-ordination, sanctions, empowerment of enforcement authorities, and cross-border enforcement co-operation.

National co-ordination

Spam impacts not only on consumer rights, data privacy, but also network security and efficiency. Consequently in most countries there is more than one agency – with different powers and priorities – which has a mandate to deal with one or more aspects of spam. For example, although the FTC is seen as having the lead enforcement role under US anti-spam legislation, this responsibility is shared with the Department of Justice (DoJ) which enforces criminal provisions of the law. This arrangement leads to the possibility of simultaneous civil and criminal proceedings against the same spammer.[46] In Italy, while the primary responsibility for the enforcement of anti-spam legislation remains with the data protection authority, it is the competition authority which is in charge of e-mail containing deceptive commercial content.

The different authorities having the responsibility over investigation and/or enforcement of the various laws that can be violated by spammers have not always been well co-ordinated to fully exploit possible synergies and to share information and resources. To overcome this problem, several countries have put in place a co-ordination mechanism: in Australia, for example, four agencies have an agreement to co-operate on spam-related matters; in the United States, the FTC has set up a domestic Spam Task Force to facilitate communication among agencies responsible for enforcing laws against spam at the federal and state level: in France the Contact Group of Anti-Spam stakeholders includes representatives of government, the regulator, the private sector and civil society; in Germany the "Alliance against Spam" was founded between the Association of the German Internet Economy (eco), the Federation of German Consumer Associations (vzbv) and the Agency to Combat Unfair Competition.

Some countries may need to increase efforts to strengthen domestic inter-agency co-operation and to designate one agency as a contact point for foreign authorities to facilitate cross border co-operation. To support this initiative, the OECD Task Force on Spam created a list of "Contact Points for national authorities" which is available on line at www.oecd-antispam.org.

Enforcement authorities – investigative powers

The power to conduct investigations and gather information and evidence is a starting point for effective enforcement policy. The evidence of illegal spam is generally electronic in nature and may be stored on many individual computers, devices, or networks in multiple countries or jurisdictions.

In this context, enforcement authorities dealing with illegal spam need appropriate search and seizure powers to preserve, access, intercept, search and seize electronic evidence. Ideally, the focus of evidence gathering should be broader than just records of message transmission, as potentially financial records and related correspondence can help determine who commissioned or was otherwise involved in generating spam. Given that spamming can easily take place from people's homes, it would be wise to ensure that some checks and external oversight are placed on the investigating authority's ability to undertake search and seizure operations. In some jurisdictions, this would be handled through the issue of warrants.

Search warrants have traditionally been issued for a particular physical location or item. However this approach is not very functional in the case of electronic evidence which presents unique issues in criminal investigations. To address these issues, and help enforcers, the Council of Europe Convention on Cybercrime provides a comprehensive procedural framework for cybercrime investigations, addressing such issues as the preservation, search and seizure of electronic evidence. Similarly, the U.S. Department of Justice, Criminal Division, Computer Crime and Intellectual Property Section, has published a comprehensive guide to searching and seizing electronic evidence.

Considering it is particularly simple for suspected spammers to arrange for the loss, destruction or concealment of pertinent electronic records which can form evidence of spam offences, it may be useful to include delayed notice provisions for search warrants.

Procedures and sanctions

The main driver for spam is the potential for economic profit. Legislation needs to foresee sanctions severe enough to discourage spam by cutting into the profit or foreseeing criminal sanctions – such as detention – for certain violations.

Sanctions are usually applied on the basis of the severity of the offence. In France marketers and online companies sending unsolicited e-mails to a number of potential customers is considered spam, however if no other violations are committed the CNIL will limit its activity to sending a warning letter, warning them that their actions are illegal, and requesting that they stop sending spam in violation of data protection laws. Consumer protection agencies usually are empowered to seek injunctions ordering the spammer to cease their activity or face penalties for contempt where spam is a vehicle for fraud.

Whenever a simple injunction or warning appears insufficient, monetary fines are usually foreseen by the legislation. Enforcement agencies, in particular data protection authorities and communication agencies, can seek monetary sanctions through administrative fines, while civil fines are applied by civil courts. The authorities can also defer the case to the criminal court, which will be able to apply criminal fines. Criminal penalties are applied in case of more severe offences, such as spam involving fraud, unauthorised use of computer resources or viruses. Penalties range from a criminal fine to detention, however the application of the latter to spammers in some countries is considered excessive, and monetary penalties are preferred.

One of the issues currently discussed is whether a private right of action is available to individual persons or corporations, to obtain meaningful statutory damages, and how civil redress can be applied to spam cases. This is of fundamental importance considering that an action against a spammer is usually time and resource intensive, and therefore private actors will not have a strong interest in pursuing the spammer unless their efforts obtain a tangible result. One of the problems in case of civil redress, however, would be the quantification of the damage caused by spam. While this could be quite straightforward in the case of fraudulent spam, which causes direct financial loss to the user, in the absence of a legislative construct it may be difficult to demonstrate that spam has caused damage or substantial cost to the affected party, or to arrange that the spammer must make sufficient restitution that they would be discouraged from sending spam in the future. Legislation could potentially be drafted to reflect the damage caused by spam, and to facilitate restitution of costs to damaged parties.

The amount of monetary sanctions, civil, criminal or administrative, may be related to the nature and gravity of the violation, and consider whether this has been repeated over time and the related circumstances (hidden or false identity, utilisation of harvested addresses, etc).[47] Sanctions can refer to each single violation, or be the result of a global evaluation of the spammer's behaviour. Australian legislation foresees the application of sanctions "in respect of each contravention", therefore virtually for each e-mail sent.[48] Countries such as Korea and Japan have already increased the amount of the sanction that can be applied to spammers. In particular, the Japanese government now allows the application of the fine directly, without the need to issue a prior "administrative order".

The table below summarise some of the remedies and sanctions available in OECD member countries.

Nature	Examples*	Comments
Civil proceedings	Monetary sanctions: Civil fine - may be a flat amount or depend on the nature and extent of the violation;. Consumer redress. Non-monetary sanctions: Warning letters; Injunctions.	Civil suit usually can be brought by: Private citizens Public and private enforcement agencies Internet Service Providers (ISPs) Fine: the amount of the sanction goes to the government Consumer redress: the money collected is returned to the victim (consumer)
Criminal proceedings	Monetary sanctions: Criminal fine. Non-monetary sanctions: Imprisonment.	Strong remedy, used in particular when the content of spam is criminal, or when the spammer did not comply with an administrative order Problem: time consuming, higher burden of proof
Administrative action	Monetary sanctions: Administrative fine. Non-monetary sanctions: Warning letters; Injunctions.	Administrative fines and other non-monetary sanctions are the primary instruments for enforcement authorities in many countries. The application of administrative remedies avoids the necessity to go through civil or criminal Courts.

* For a more detailed analysis see the enforcement report, DSTI/CP/ICCP/SPAM(2004)3/FINAL at: http://www.oecd-antispam.org/rubrique.php3?id_rubrique=8.

Co-operation and information sharing

Like many problems related to activities conducted via the Internet spam raises problems of enforcement of national laws. Spammers who are apparently breaching the laws of a particular country may well be located in different geographic locations.

The regulation of spam and the enforcement of spam laws are complicated by difficulties associated with the collection and preservation of evidence in cases where spam crosses national borders requiring co-operation between a domestic agency and its foreign counterpart in order to prosecute.

If national anti-spam regulation explicitly supports regulators to assist their counterparts in other countries in gathering evidence for investigations, the efficacy of co-operative arrangements will be greatly enhanced. Equally, the development of standardised approaches for gathering and providing electronic evidence, with a particular recognition of privacy issues involved in the cross-border transmission of evidence, may aid the enforcement of not just the jurisdiction's spam legislation, but also of other laws pertaining to online crime.

Several Memoranda of Understanding (MoUs) and informal co-operation agreements have been developed in the past years between a number of OECD countries, often on a bilateral basis; they are usually "best effort" agreements, concluded between a limited number of entities. The various existing instruments show that anti-spam regulators – from both OECD and non-OECD countries – can co-operate with goodwill at the working level.

Certain arrangements have facilitated co-operation, to ensure better co-ordination between stakeholders. The London Action Plan (LAP) combines enforcement agencies and industry to create a multilateral network for international anti-spam enforcement. Francophone networks[49] are currently working on a French speaking multilateral network for international anti-spam co-operation.

In addition, different projects stemming from research centers, such as "Spotspam" and "Signal-spam" encourage the exchange of information and co-ordination efforts between the private and public sectors. The French project "Signal-Spam" in particular, ensures the technical and operational management of software for collecting, flagging and analysing spam. The resulting information is then re-directed to the appropriate bodies to rapidly respond and terminate the spammer's action.

At the EU level the contact network of spam enforcement authorities (CNSA) was set up at the initiative of the Commission following its Communication of January 2004. The CNSA facilitates the sharing of information and best practices in enforcing anti-spam laws between the national authorities of EU Member States. In addition, a voluntary agreement was drawn up in February 2005 to establish a common procedure for handling cross-border complaints on spam.[50]

Following discussions in their respective *fora*, the LAP and the CNSA recently developed a "Spam Complaint Referral" pro forma and accompanying guidance (see annex V) which has been used by some LAP and/or CNSA authorities[51]. The pro forma and guidance are working documents which facilitate the request for assistance and the referral of a spam investigation to another participating authority. These documents are subject to review and revision.

In addition, existing criminal law enforcement co-operation networks (such as the G8 24/7 Network) and mutual legal assistance instruments (such as mutual legal assistance treaties and letters rogatory procedures), already allow countries to co-operate and share information in furtherance of criminal investigations and prosecutions involving criminal spam and other forms of cybercrime.

Cross-border enforcement co-operation

On the basis of the above findings, it is apparent that enforcement action across borders would benefit from a global strategy to overcome a number of challenges, such as information gathering and sharing, identification of enforcement priorities, and development of an effective international enforcement framework. To this end, an OECD Council Recommendation was adopted in order to provide guidance and advice on how to improve cross-border co-operation in the enforcement of laws against spam (Annex I)[52] On the basis of the recommendation, governments should improve their legislation in order to:

a) Establish a domestic framework to empower national enforcement authorities to investigate and take action against spam.

b) Improve the ability of authorities to co-operate with their foreign counterparts, providing national bodies with the possibility to share relevant information and provide investigative assistance.

c) Improve procedures for co-operation, prioritising requests for assistance and making use of common resources and networks.[53]

d) Develop new co-operative models between Enforcement authorities and relevant private sector entities.

ELEMENT III – INDUSTRY DRIVEN INITIATIVE

> The nature and the rapid evolution of the Internet has provoked a change in the respective roles of governments, industries and users in the online economy, and created interest in the concept of self-regulation.

As mentioned in the previous sections, government regulation and legislation is indeed fundamental as a basis for combating spam, but legislation is not always sufficiently flexible to deal with rapid technological changes, nor is it always effective in dealing with the complexities of cross-border enforcement, difficulties encountered in identifying spammers, etc. To appropriately deal with spam on the Internet the generally-applicable anti-spam laws in countries should be coupled with self-regulatory initiatives undertaken by private sector players, such as Internet Service Providers, telecommunication operators, direct marketers, online operators, software companies, and their associations.

Internet Service Providers

Governments and regulators have usually supported a hands-off self-regulatory approach for ISPs, which are not held responsible for the content and data that traverse their networks, as it was feared that imposing responsibility on ISPs would lead to a stricter oversight on content, and therefore to greater online censorship.

Nevertheless, ISPs play a central role in the field of Internet security, and the idea that messaging providers should actively intervene to prevent spam from being sent from or across their networks is gaining acceptance. This is because while many ISPs are already actively combating spam, some are lagging behind, and without the adoption and implementation of a harmonised set of rules (e.g. code of conduct, best practices) there is not a guarantee that they will work to impede the utilisation of their services by spammers, and provide adequate educational and technical tools to their users to appropriately address the threats posed by spam, spybots, botnets, computer hijacking, etc.

Generally, there are no provisions in national legislative instruments imposing any kind of obligation on ISPs to intervene actively to help eliminate spam, nonetheless most of the providers have a commercial interest in blocking/limiting incoming spam to protect their customers, as the massive presence of spam would disrupt their service, affecting its availability and reliability. The provision of spam filters could therefore work as a competitive advantage for ISPs, which will be able to offer enhanced services, and therefore attract more users. Anti-spam features are increasingly included in ISPs packages, in particular with broadband connections. Although important for users, blocking incoming spam may not necessarily help reduce the overall volume of spam generated and may well lead to an increase in this volume, as spammers seek to maintain their revenues by contacting a larger number of potential customers.

Outbound spam impacts more indirectly customers by reducing quality of service and slowing network response time by using up a part of the provider's capacity. In addition, third-party providers may decide to block all messages originating from an ISP repeatedly used by spammers, by using public "blacklists" of IP addresses or domains. This practice can serve as a deterrent to stop providers from engaging in so called "pink contracts".[54] and as a stimulus to take action to avoid the misuse of their resources. Blacklists, however, have several shortcomings, which are analysed in the section on Technical Solutions.

Technical measures and self-regulation

Internet service providers and network operators can contribute to combating spam on two different fronts: on the technological side, they may develop and apply technology solutions to limit or block not only the receiving, but directly the sending of spam messages. On the operational side, they are in the position to implement a code of conduct for ISPs and to impose on their customers Acceptable Use Policy (AUPs) forbidding spam (Box 2).

Discussion regarding the role of ISPs vis-à-vis the problem of spam was initiated in the IETF (Internet Engineering Task Force) framework, through a memo titled "Email submission between independent networks".[55] The document, aimed at improving lines of accountability for controlling abusive users of the Internet mail services, suggested a series of best practices/behaviour that ISPs sending or receiving e-mails from other ISPs should follow.

Similarly, the Anti-Spam Technical Alliance (ASTA), a collaborative effort between some of the leading Internet providers and the Internet community, active until 2004, was created to establish technical and non-technical solutions for handling unsolicited commercial e-mail. The alliance created a "Technology and Policy Proposal", which was issued in June 2004,[56] and included a series of best practices and technical approaches that ISPs should adopt in order to control abusive traffic thus reducing the chances for a spammer to (mis)use their servers to send unsolicited messages. These techniques are based on "Good Neighbour" policies, i.e. ISPs are responsible for controlling the traffic they originate.

Given the link between spam and network security, providers, besides using filters to block the reception of spam, should also improve security on their network, to avoid becoming a source of spam. Many providers hold the view that the problem of "botnets"[57] and "zombies" can be solved, or at least limited, by implementing security best practices, applying AUPs and educating users to employ available tools to protect their computers.[58]

Box 2. Acceptable Use Policy (AUPs)[59]

Several messaging providers include in their Term of Service, accepted by the user, a series of rules on how the service can be used, what is unacceptable behaviour, and the consequences of any eventual breach. Typical user policies (applied consistently by a large number of providers) include prohibition to:

- Send, transmit, distribute or deliver unsolicited bulk or unsolicited commercial e-mail (spam).
- Forge e-mails headers or otherwise manipulate identifiers in order to disguise the origin of any content transmitted through the service.
- Terms of services also warn users that in case of violation the ISP will have the right to take, without notice, actions deemed appropriate, such as blocking messages from a particular Internet domain, mail server or IP address or immediately terminate any account on any service which has been used to transmit any message that violates this policy. Unacceptable utilisation often includes address harvesting, illegal and harmful content, spam sent to mailing lists and newsletters.
- Some providers have taken a more comprehensive approach, and their user policies include not only e-mails, but any kind of practice to upload, post, e-mail, transmit or otherwise make available any unsolicited or unauthorised advertising, promotional material or any other form of solicitation (except in areas designated for this purpose).
- The sending of messages that contain software viruses or any other malicious code or program designed to damage the functionality of any computer software or hardware or telecommunication equipment is forbidden in most cases.

The ASTA Technology and Policy proposal included a series of best practices and technologies that ISPs should implement to help secure the e-mail infrastructure and bring about increased accountability. However, the document recognises that technical solutions are not "the" solution to the spam problem, and acknowledges that provisions must be flexible and ready to change to adapt to the rapidly evolving Internet environment and its vulnerabilities. For this reason governments are refraining from imposing technological solutions on ISPs, and ISPs associations and alliances prefer to concentrate more generally on agreeing on best practices and objectives, rather than setting up specific rules. A typical example of this approach is the Code of Conduct adopted by the Messaging Anti-Abuse Working Group (MAAWG),[60] an organisation now including almost all former ASTA members, and continuing the technical work initiated there.

Not all ISPs, however, seem to be aware of, or particularly concerned by, spam and security issues. In this context the US Federal Trade Commission, together with other partners from around the world, launched in January 2004 "*Operation Secure Your Server*", with the aim to let individuals and organisations know that their mail servers or proxy servers can be abused by spammers, and to provide information on how servers can be secured to avoid further abuses by spammers. Although open relays and open proxies still exist, other spamming techniques have emerged. In this context the FTC and its international partners, in the framework of the London Action Plan activities, launched "*Operation Spam Zombies*" in 2005, aimed at reducing the phenomenon of "zombies" or hijacked computers.

A "zombie" is a machine – typically connected to a broadband connection – that has been maliciously infected by a worm or virus without the owners' knowledge, and is used for purposes such as to launch Denial of Service (DoS) attacks and send spam and phishing e-mails. These computers form a network which provides greater combined processing power for spammers, at the same time draining e-mail server resources. The consulting company Sophos, in its 2005 report, affirmed that compromised PCs are responsible for 40% of the world's spam. In May 2005 Ciphertrust affirmed that an average of 172,009 new zombies were identified each day, mainly from the United States, China and Korea. European countries have also been affected by zombies, with France, Germany and the United Kingdom accounting in May 2005 for 14% of identified zombies.[61] Data from MessageLabs in October 2004 highlighted that 79% of spam came from "open proxy," computers or zombie botnets. The same tests for February 2005 indicated that spam from these sources declined to 59%, although the total volume of spam did not decrease in the same proportion.

Within the "*Operation Spam Zombies*"[62] about 30 economies were engaged in contacting ISPs around the world to urge them to:

i) Block port 25, except in certain circumstances.

ii) Apply rate-limiting controls for e-mail relays.

iii) Identify computers that are sending atypical amounts of e-mail, and take steps to determine if the computer is acting as a spam zombie; when necessary, quarantine the affected computer until the source of the problem is removed.

iv) Give customers plain language advice. And

v) Point customers to tools to remove zombie code.

There is no universal consensus, however, on the first measure, *i.e.* blocking port 25. A number of ISPs, while willing to contribute to co-operative initiatives, are reluctant to take the responsibility for monitoring and fixing compromised computers in their networks.

Internet access providers are in a position to exert some control on the transmission of data. For this reason, the Report of the Canadian Task Force on Spam highlighted that ISPs had a fundamental role in anti-spam solutions.[63] ISPs could take action through specific provisions against spam in the ISP AUPs, but also by adopting recommended best practices and technical solutions to limit inbound and outbound spam: in the framework of the OECD Task Force on spam Toolkit, BIAC and MAAWG developed a set of recommended best practices for ISPs and network operators (Annex II).

Technical solutions, as well as policy issues relating to spam are also addressed by the MAAWG and EmailAuthentication.org, which have been established to improve co-operation among a group of communication and technology companies. The MAAWG, which includes among its members AOL, Bell Canada, Comcast, EarthLink, France Telecom, Microsoft and Yahoo, is working on collaboration among ISPs, technology, and public policy. The Emailauthentication.org was jointly created by the Direct Marketing Association (DMA), Email Service Providers Coalition, Microsoft, Bigfoot, Symantec, and Sendmail, and obtained the support of the anti-phishing working group, Yahoo and others. The association aims at facilitating the deployment and implementation of e-mail authentication standards and solutions. To this end it organised the Email Authentication Implementation Summit, which took place in New York city in July 2005. MAAWG also issued in July 2005 its whitepaper on SPF/SenderID deployment guidelines, and in November 2005 its Recommendation on port 25 management.[64] Guidelines for inter-operator communications have also been established by MAAWG, such as spam feedback loops and operational contact networks.

In particular, it has been suggested that messaging operators should establish a set of policies which defines permissible and prohibited uses of their services. These policies can be included in the Terms of Service or in the Acceptable User Policy (AUP), which are endorsed by customers at the conclusion of the contract with the provider. The infringement of these policies results in a breach of contract, giving the operator the right to suspend the service or terminate the account.

The code of conduct also considers the position of a messaging operator vis-à-vis inbound mails. Operators should indeed try to limit the amount of outbound unsolicited messages from their servers, but also be able to protect their servers, networks, users and other applicable resources from abuse by other operator's systems. This implies the possibility of taking protective measures to prevent the abusive messaging system from accessing their resources.

Banks and other online operators

In the context of fraudulent and deceptive spam messages and phishing scams, online operators also have an important role to play. Phishing frauds (see Introduction), for example, circulate through spam e-mails which appear as a legitimate message from an online service, such as a bank, an online seller, etc. The possibility to be misled by such messages is elevated as online companies, while increasingly using electronic messages to communicate with their users, rarely have a standardised and clear set of rules regarding which kind of information will or will not be sent by e-mail, which formal elements will be included in the message, and how users can identify and report false and fraudulent communications.

To this end, several companies developed – or are in the process of developing – internal policies and guidelines to respond and effectively prevent phishing attacks. The areas where a company has control and can take action are multiple and include:[65]

- **Corporate communication methods and standards**: following company standards for Web sites, domain usage and e-mail messaging makes it harder for a phisher to fool victims. Clear company e-mail policies – such as never asking for personal information or possibly never providing a clickable link in an e-mail – must be established and applied consistently. A company sending out e-mail to its customer may consider a means to authenticate them or use digital signatures.

- **Pre-emptive activities** to create barriers to phishing and make it difficult for scammers to prepare attacks. These include measures to make the company's Web site less vulnerable to brand attacks by using clear domain name and defensive domain registration (*i.e.* register domain names which are similar to the company's own domain and may create confusion), Web site usage monitoring, control of "bounced" messages, monitoring of look-alike sites, etc.

- **Consumer education** and awareness, customer support. Online operators should communicate effectively with their customers. They should clarify which kind of communications can/will be sent by e-mail, specify that the user will never be asked to provide their personal data via e-mail, and list elements users need to verify in the message to be sure it is from the online operator.

Currently e-mail policies are different and the amount of information and warning provided varies. For these reasons it would be advisable for banks and financial institutes, but also for online operators in general, which use e-mails as a communication tool with customers, to develop a list of clear and harmonised e-mailing best practices, which should be part of the broader approach to security.

Industry associations

Codes of conduct and best practices are usually developed in the framework of industry associations, which are proliferating in the ICT sector. Telecommunication operators, software providers, manufacturers, Internet service providers, often join associations which have the goal to promote common interest, harmonise their approaches and exchange best practices, facilitate co-operation, and face together some of the main problems affecting the technology/service they are dealing with. There are a number of national associations of Internet Service Providers such as the *Association des Fournisseurs d'Access* (AFA) the Australian Internet Industry Association (IIA), the German ISP Association ECO, and the Canadian Association of Internet Providers, which are particularly active in this field.

At the regional level, EuroISPA is the European association of national ISPs associations.[66] EuroISPA aims to take a co-ordinated approach to Internet services at the European level, to represent the sector's interests at European institutions, and to provide an interface between providers and other parts of the industry, such as direct marketing associations. EuroISPA is involved with the EU funded project "spotspam" initiative, proposed by ECO, the German member of the association. The project aims to facilitate evidence gathering and exchange of information where legal action is taken against a spammer, and to provide a supranational source of information to monitor spam complaints.[67] EuroISPA is also providing resources to its members, supporting information exchange and the utilisation of best practices.

To address threats closely linked to spam messages, the Anti-Phishing Working Group, an industry association of software providers, security solutions developers and online operators, was created to provide a resource for information and warning and to suggest possible measures to deal with phishing and e-mail frauds.[68] The APWG Web site is an important source of data and warning on new phishing and pharming attacks, provides statistics on the growth and evolution of the phenomenon, and has a members' area in which participants can post documents, ask questions and discuss new issues.

Online marketers and operators using bulk e-mail advertising are mostly concerned by anti-spam measures, as they need to be sure their messages respect anti-spam legislation and gets through the growing number of anti-spam filters to the user/customer inbox. To this end, direct marketing associations have developed codes of conduct the adhesion to which provides a guarantee of fair trading, and respect of the relevant legislative provisions. An example is the Australian DMA code of conduct, limiting unsolicited e-mail advertising, or the "*codes de bonne pratique*" implemented by the French DMAs (UFMD and SNCD), which have been endorsed by the CNIL. Codes and best practices do not only establish rules members have to follow, but also provide a step-by-step guide to planning and implementing online marketing activities.[69] In the framework of the OECD Task Force on spam Toolkit, BIAC developed a set of recommended best practices for e-mail marketers, which are available in Annex III.

Although mobile phone marketing, at the moment, is not as developed as e-mail marketing – mainly due to the cost of sending SMS, the phenomenon is developing to include voice files, SMS, MMS, WAP messaging, and Java, SyncML and video and audio messaging–however it could grow in the future thanks to the improvement of wireless connections such as Bluetooth, Ultra Wide Band (UWB), etc. These new tools provide new opportunities and features to users; they also present a higher risk of violation of consumers' privacy and security. For this reason, for example, Vodafone K.K. Japan in 2005 implemented

SMS sending limitations.[70] The UK branch of the Mobile Marketing Association (MMA), an industry trade association for companies involved in mobile marketing and associated technologies, elaborated in 2003 a code of conduct and best practices guidelines for the industry.[71]

The code provides guidance to developing activity within the framework of current legislation as well as referencing guidelines from other industry bodies, such as the ASA, DMA and ICSTIS. It also includes information/wording that needs to be included in these communications, specific rules for the marketing relating to particular types of products and services, and marketing to children. In addition, conditions are set for location based mobile marketing, and marketing using premium rate numbers. Other MMA member countries are developing their codes, following the principles at the basis of the UK document.[72]

From the mobile operators' side, the GSM Association, in order to address problems regarding inter-operator or cross-border spam practices, developed a mobile Spam Code of Practice (see Annex IV) which should include technical and legal measures that can be considered by mobile operators to fight spam (see Box 3). In this framework, operators also call for governments and consumer associations to take action by supporting the development of industry self-regulation mechanism and responsible mobile marketing and premium rate industries. Similarly to what happen in the case of e-mail spam, government has an important role to assist mobile operators, for example by reviewing national legislation that may inhibit anti-spam activities and by considering what steps they can take to prevent spammers from profiting financially from such activities. Also, national authorities can support investigations on spam abuses and fraud, and remove obstacles to the operator's ability to investigate mobile spam cases.

Box 3. Mobile operators[73]

Measures and approaches that can be considered by mobile operators for combating mobile spam include:

- Develop a clear anti-spam policy that prohibits the use of mobile networks for initiating or sending mobile spam.
- Include anti-spam conditions in third party contracts.
- Provide customers with information, advice and resources for dealing with mobile spam including facilities for reporting suspected incidents of mobile spam.
- Monitor networks for signs of mobile spam and establish procedures for prioritising and dealing with suspected incidents.
- Adopt recommended techniques for detecting and dealing with mobile spam and fraudulent messages.
- Co-operate with other mobile operators to minimise mobile spam sent across networks and share information on best practice.

The role of private stakeholders

It is clear that private stakeholders have an active role to play in reducing spam, by implementing appropriate policies, and applying technological solutions which would impede spam from circulating in networks.

The application of codes of conduct and best practices on the side of online operators could help in guaranteeing that legitimate messages are delivered, thus increasing the availability of the service, and help users distinguish between a real message and an identity theft attempt via e-mail (phishing). The adoption of harmonised rules among the different categories of players could have a substantial role in building a comprehensive anti-spam framework. It is not a question of responsibility, but a question of who is best placed to act.

ELEMENT IV – ANTI-SPAM TECHNOLOGIES

Introduction

Spam presents complex technical challenges, and therefore solutions to eliminating it need to be supported by appropriate technical measures. While government action and legislation are fundamental, they are insufficient to meet the challenges posed by spam, viruses and spyware. In addition, the Internet structure makes it particularly difficult for enforcers to identify spammers, and therefore to punish them.

The nature of spam does not lend itself to easy definition. Despite problems of definition, however, there are both technologies and techniques that can be used to help control the problem of unwanted e-mails. This section is meant to provide a neutral overview of the various types of technological tools and methods as well as factors to consider prior to their implementation.[74] It refers specifically to tools as opposed to solutions. While technology is designed to address many of the problems created by spam, and may in fact "solve" some of the specific issues related to spam, an overall solution to spam can only be achieved through a multifactor approach that includes technology, policy (including regulation where appropriate), practice, and education.

Anti-spam tools operate at many levels – point of origination, in the backbone, at the gateway and on the recipient computer – and may be used alone or in combination. Updated information and resources are available on the Toolkit Web site at www.oecd-antispam.org.[75]

This section is addressed in particular to mail server managers, in order to provide them with an insight into the strong and weak points of each filtering technique, to enable them to choose software according to their e-mail policy and needs, depending upon their planned architecture. The focus of the section is on practices for incoming mail, while practices aimed at reducing outgoing spam have not been considered.

Tools that deal with spam need to focus on both the mail and on the behaviour surrounding the mail. In light of these multiple factors, many instruments and methods are based on sets of rules or assumptions that work alone or in combination to identify suspect e-mails. Over time, spam has grown in scope to include more viruses and malware. This requires defensive technology to go beyond the text-based tools to tools that analyse behavioural and contextual factors in determining whether to accept or reject specific mail or even attempted connections. Considering the increased security threat presented by spam, we expect that anti-spam technologies will either contain more, or need to work in conjunction with, advanced security and authentication technologies.

The importance of tool/technology context

Some of the tools/technologies considered in this section are specifically designed to be implemented at the entrance to the e-mail platform, whereas others can be more usefully deployed after the receipt of messages but prior to delivery to the end user. At each stage of filter application, the aim of implementing a rule may be to refuse or reject the electronic message, or simply to mark it or deliver it to the end user's spam box.

The relevance and usefulness of each rule can therefore only be judged in terms of the precise context in which it is applied, the level at which it is applied in the message distribution process, and what finally happens to the communication.

Combining tests

Judicious application of technology should be the backbone of any approach that aims to defeat spam. One should be aware that none of the technologies discussed in the following will act as a "silver bullet" or one-stop solution to the problems created by spam. Rather, all of the technologies are complementary and will be most effective when implemented in conjunction with each other. The integration of a number of technologies is necessary to reduce the harmful impact of spam on a system.

The attention of administrators is drawn to the fact that tests are not necessarily to be used in "all or nothing" mode. On the contrary, it is preferable to combine tests to maximise the number of spam e-mails intercepted while minimising the number of legitimate e-mails inadvertently intercepted or refused.

- All or nothing refusal – this is one possible response from services using a black list. Any message that fails the test is refused. The occurrence of the error does depend, however, on where the rule is located in the distribution process.

- Access privilege – this is one possible response from servers using a white list. Any message that passes the test is accepted. There is no risk of a legitimate message being rejected, but there may be false negatives. For example, a domain white list is of no real interest if the sender's domain is not authenticated (with Sender Policy Framework or DomainKeys Identified Mail, DKIM).

- Many spam messages or worms claim to originate from recognised consumer brands in the hope of gaining access privilege.

- Scoring – this is how programs such as SpamAssassin (and also procmail) combine their tests. Avoiding the inconveniences of "all or nothing", scoring is highly recommended. However, it is costly in terms of machine resources and the continued requirement of updating scoring factors to maximise hits while minimising false positives.

The conventional method is to run several "all or nothing" tests and then score the messages that have been allowed in.

The recommended good practice is to combine several techniques, but not so many that the resultant complexity creates an unreliable mail delivery system.

Types of anti-spam technologies

Authentication of electronic mail

The first comment that needs to be made is that mail authentication methods fall into the category of rules, which, although they help in the fight against spam, do not constitute specific anti-spam technologies.

An analogy may help to make this clear. Identity cards are not a "trust marker" in that perpetrators may also have an identity card. The requirement for transparency, however, will be of greater benefit to legitimate senders than to spammers.

SPF and/or Sender-ID

A major force behind the proliferation of spam is the ability of spammers to hide the true return address of their messages. The architecture of electronic mail does not imply a prior contact between the sender and the recipient. Therefore, it is not possible to rely on systematic authentication. The problem is of growing concern because forged addresses have been used in phishing scams that lure message recipients into disclosing credit card numbers and other personal information.

The application of this technology is still emerging and therefore lacks standardisation, but authentication works by flagging or blocking e-mail messages whose true senders cannot be verified. The key advantage of sender authentication is that it places the burden of spam dissemination on the sender rather than on the receiver and renders phishing attacks more difficult. The increased costs for senders are offset by guaranteed message delivery if senders are authenticated and are using the system legitimately. The specifics of the verification process vary with the model chosen, and several server authentication models currently exist. Two of the most prevalent are Sender Policy Framework (SPF) and Sender-ID.

These two techniques can be discussed together because they share several common features. The question of which one to choose, however, is less straightforward.

SPF and Sender-ID can be used to test whether an e-mail server is authorised to send on behalf of a given domain. This is done by publishing a record in the Domain Name System (DNS), which lists the authorized e-mail servers for a domain. The two techniques primarily differ in the choice of the identity tested. SPF tests the envelope's MAIL FROM (2821), while Sender-ID tests the headers (2822).

Server administrators take two types of action - they publish SPF records in the DNS and they test them on entry.

Few domains currently publish SPF records, with the result that interest in it is limited. Some administrators note that Sender-ID is a new concept and has not yet been widely tested. The two techniques are not yet based on a stable standard.

The authentication of electronic mail by checking the IP addresses of the sender's server will help to reduce and manage spam in the future. This will probably call for the creation of services above authentication, for example private white lists, reputation services, and accreditation services.

Issues for consideration: SPF and Sender-ID can be tested on entry. Because these are emerging tools, users are cautioned against too much reliance on them until further uptake, unless otherwise indicated by the remote server or the particular context. Authentication is a critical component in any mail security procedure. SPF is currently the most widespread technique. Publishing SPF and Sender ID records is also recommended.

DKIM /or META

DKIM and Message Enhancements for Transmission Authorization (META) are used to authenticate the sender domain by means of a cryptographic signature automatically added by the e-mail server. At present, the immediate practical benefits are very low since few domains sign their messages. Furthermore, administrators will note that these three techniques are not yet based on a stable standard.

The authentication of electronic mail by cryptographic signature of the message should help to reduce and manage spam in the future.

DKIM is the most publicised of these models. The model works by requiring a digital signature, or private key, on all outbound messages. The incoming messages are authenticated at the domain and mail server levels by ensuring that the private key matches the public key already on file. This method ensures that the message could only have come from the originating ISP.

Issues for consideration: These techniques can be studied and tested. It should be noted that they are emerging technologies, and, pending further large-scale deployment, it may be premature to rely on them at the present juncture.

Existence of the sender's domain and eliciting a response

Many spammers send mail with a non-existent sender's address. A rule can be used to refuse these messages, such as the Postfix directive reject_unknown_sender_domain or the j-chkmail directive BadMX. Another possibility is to verify the validity of the record for the incoming server (MX) for the domain given in the "from" field of the message. Some spammers set up a dummy MX record to avoid angry replies of protest (for instance, the MX goes to 127.0.0.1, which means the local sender).

These rules call for a small amount of DNS traffic, which probably would have occurred anyway during the reply, and they can also reject a certain amount of spam.

Issues for consideration:	This technique is not widely used. The annoyance is minimal in that, if the sender's domain does not exist, it will be difficult (although not impossible, thanks to the automatic function of Reply-To) to reply to the message. "No reply" send boxes should not be used.

Existence of a Pointer Record (PTR)

A PTR record of the DNS can be used to translate the IP address of the sender's server into a name, although without necessarily checking that this name is consistent with the sender's domain.

The addition of such records is not always under the control of the sender's domain (if there is no addr.arpa delegation by the IP, for example), which, even if it is legitimate, may be unable to meet the obligation. These records can be used to determine the source of an e-mail message and whether or to what extent it can be trusted. They can also be used to determine whether a mail originates from a residential IP address or to redeliver an error message to the right server.

Issues for consideration:	This test can prove useful in order to indicate in the header of the e-mail that the field is empty or suspect (for example it did not lead to an IP when directly requested). The PTR field can still be useful (particularly if the remote server agrees) to return certain information to the recipient. However, using this test to refuse an electronic message for the sole reason that the PTR field of the connecting IP has no content should be avoided. The utilisation of this test to refuse an electronic message should also be avoided unless circumstances (e.g. if the field can be used to determine the origin of the message) or policy (e.g. refusal of messages from particular residential IPs) dictate it.

Blacklists/Whitelists

Traditional filtering as well as tracking complaints across user communities can ultimately lead to whitelists of acceptable senders and blacklists of suspected spammers. The whitelist/blacklist approach is often a too drastic solution to be acceptable by most users. Whitelists are time-consuming to create and will require continual updating. Blacklists require similar monitoring. All lists need mechanisms and procedures for updating to address false positives and fraudulent complaints to a listing. Spoofing and open relays can also create issues related to the appearance that mail has originated from a source.

Blacklists are based on the principle of listing sources of spam. This list can include the names of machines, IP addresses or electronic addresses. It can be implemented by an entity for shared use, or introduced and maintained by the server using it for its own requirements.

With current Mail Transfer Agents (MTAs), this test can be carried out in the SMTP session and therefore result in rejection even before the message is sent. Some lists contain open relays that do not send spam alone. Their open relay configuration can be treated as illegitimate behaviour by the platforms to which messages are sent

The quality of blacklists varies enormously, depending on the professionalism of the compiler. Many lists are poorly managed, abandoned, or of dubious integrity: names can be added quickly, the applied criteria may be unclear, and the removal from the list may be virtually impossible or be operated only on a payment basis. This problem is mainly due to the absence of a code of conduct or any kind of regulation to discipline and limit the functioning of blacklists. If this solution is to be used in the future, a co-operative effort to establish a list of good practices, clearly establishing cases in which addresses can be blacklisted and the conditions under which they will be removed from the lists, is necessary.

Blacklists will inevitably contain inaccuracies that will prevent some legitimate messages from getting through to the consumer. This problem, known as the false positive problem, has led to legal disputes when legitimate senders believed they were erroneously placed on an ISP's black list. Further, the false positive problem for individual users can result in a serious drawback of relying solely on traditional filtering technology to stop spam.

Although their utilization raises many concerns, blacklists are a quick solution to refuse a connection to machines whose behaviour endangers the security or quality of services of the platform to which mail is sent, or to reject messages from certain senders.

Issues for consideration: **Care should be taken in choosing lists**. Before choosing a list, it would be advisable to consider a few points:

- Use lists that are well managed.
- Ensure that there is a professional administrator who replies and reacts.
- Addition and removal criteria are clear, reasonable and accessible.

When an external list is used, its activity needs to be monitored because quality evolves over time. If an administrator manages his own black list (which is resource-intense), the above criteria for quality will obviously also apply. Since it is difficult to provide a rapid summary of black lists, given their variety, a cautious approach has to be recommended.

Address of the sending server treated as either "dynamic" or "residential"

This is a particular form of blacklist in which the criterion for addition to the list is the fact that the IP address being blocked corresponds to the machine of an individual subscriber to an ISP and not to the mail server of an organisation. The idea is that an ordinary subscriber does not send mail directly in SMTP, but passes through the PTA of his provider. This typically means the machine being blocked is directly sending spam messages from a spammer, or more commonly that the messages are being sent without the owner's knowledge (i.e. the machine has been compromised and turned into a "zombie" in order to send the messages).

The lists of such addresses are not always reliable since most of them have been compiled using heuristics, such as the presence of "adsl" in the name of the machine. Managing such lists is also resource-intensive.

In contrast, some of these lists, notably those compiled by the server using them, can be used to distinguish between servers authorised for a domain and the residential lists. Moreover, some domains publish the ranges of residential addresses for their domain.

This test can be seen as discriminating between "pure consumers" and "providers". The latter consider legitimate the policy by which the owner of a domain refuses to connect his machines to residential addresses, as these are currently the main source of spam. Consumers however argue that spam exists and the freedom to use e-mail must be protected.

Filtering

Filtering is the most common technical anti-spam technology. The main benefits of filters are the ease of implementation and the flexibility that users have in deciding which messages should be treated as spam. Heuristic filters require that users specify criteria, such as keywords or a sender's address that will prompt the filter to block certain messages from reaching the consumer's inbox. Spammers who deliberately misspell words or spell them in a different language easily outsmart the keyword approach. Bayesian filters are based on experience. They create statistics about the messages in a recognition table for future reference for individual users to distinguish between spam and legitimate mails. The filter then lets through only messages that resemble the user's previous legitimate mail.

Heuristic filters

These filters are based on the principle of testing for the presence in the message of certain typical features of spam, such as the exclusive use of HTML or the type of customer to whom the mail is sent. The test is weighted through a learning process based on a set of known spam mails and a set of mails known to be legitimate (the scores are therefore not calculated by a human in order to reduce subjectivity). One of the most well-known and widely used filters is SpamAssassin. Yahoo!, Hotmail, and AOL, among others, use heuristic filters in their junk-mail filtering systems.

These filters carry the risk that a message using spammer techniques – spectacular messages in HTML, for example – will be classified as spam. Furthermore, it should be noted that the filters use large amounts of machine resources.

These filters can detect a high proportion of spam mail, and they do not need to be taught or configured. However, since they use a large number of tests, it is best to be aware that it is possible to change which tests are run and the scores used to classify messages as spam.

Issues for consideration:	Easy for users to install, these filters offer a high degree of filtering for little work by the administrator. Care must be taken to regularly update the test base, as in the case of anti-virus programs. A two-year old anti-spam program may hardly catch any spam as the latter has now evolved. Potential for false positives must be monitored, and filter criteria must be adjusted. Also, some of these filters implemented at the B2B level have the ability to provide notice to the recipient of certain suppressions to allow a review of whether it was properly classified.

Keyword filters

These are binary filters that search for a keyword ("Viagra," etc.). The risk of false positives is very high and the ability to avoid these by spacing, alternate characters and misspelling is also substantial.

Issues for consideration:	Keyword filters lack granularity and effectiveness unless they are specifically relevant to the context in which they are used.

Summary or fingerprint filters

Fingerprint filters, such as Razor, construct a fingerprint of the message submitted to them and indicate whether it has already been identified as spam. There are many false negatives because a number of types of spam mail are not identified even when the server scans them with Razor. Furthermore, the message sometimes varies sufficiently for it to generate a different fingerprint. One solution to this problem is to delay the mail (as greylisting does). They generate few false positives.

Bayesian filters

By way of an opening comment, it should be noted that the techniques described do not concern personal configurations on end-user machines but rather those of a group server.

The principle on which the Bayesian filter works is to prime its engine by examining a set of known spam e-mails and a set of e-mails known to be legitimate, then after teaching itself the vocabulary used by spammers from this known list it will use Bayesian probabilities to calculate whether a message is spam. In the case of a group filter, the learning is usually conducted by the system administrator.

Being based on the concept of spam vocabulary, these filters can pose problems when used on a shared basis. In a small-scale and highly uniform environment (for example a firm or a University department in which everyone works in the same domain with similar vocabularies), this may be acceptable. However, this would undoubtedly not be the case for a major e-mail provider and particularly a public provider unless the group base offers each individual user the possibility of customising the filter for his/her own mailbox. The problem is that what is acceptable vocabulary to some users may trigger the filter if it has been deemed by the group to be spammer vocabulary.

Despite potential issues at the group level, these filters are highly effective when used by individual users and are one of the few solutions which, when used alone, can filter out almost all spam mails after suitable training. Microsoft provides customisable Bayesian filtering in Outlook and Exchange Server. Another example is the free program Bogofilter (www.bogofilter.org).

Issues for consideration:	These filters should be used on an individual basis or allow users to customise them.

Behavioural filters

This type of filter examines the behaviour of the remote server, such as the number of mails sent by unit of time. Rate limiting is one example of this type of filtering. The idea is that ordinary mails are only sent individually or in very small numbers and spam mails are sent in very large batches.

This type of filter is extremely delicate because typically there is no way to distinguish between a spammer and a legitimate distribution list server, such as a newsgroup.

According to some experts, it is nonetheless legitimate for a platform to refuse certain volumes of mail, primarily due to its size or its mission to ensure the security of its networks. It would also seem legitimate to ask bulk mail senders to respect the resources of the remote platform by bearing the cost of distributing their messages without trying to send them too quickly in order to free themselves from the costs inherent in using e-mails as a channel of communication.

Issues for consideration: Depending upon the policy of the recipient, this type of filter can be used either to restrict flow rates or to block incoming mails. In the latter case, an explanation of the reason for the reject must be accessible by the sender so that the latter can comply with the distribution criteria.

HELO/CSV

A sending computer identifies itself by name to a receiving computer at the beginning of each SMTP transaction. The SMTP command the sending computer uses to identify itself by this name to the receiving computer is called the "EHLO" or "HELO" command.

Certified Server Validation (CSV) is a service that provides a mechanism for a mail-receiving server to assess a mail-sending server. It builds upon the existing practice of service providers that accredit the networks from which sending systems are connecting.

HELO tests check that the remote MTA is properly configured, but these tests do not indicate whether it is a spammer or not. CSV tests add a probability test on the name: does it really correspond to a domain? Unlike SPF or DKIM, CSV does not authenticate the domain sending the message but rather the domain of the e-mail server (which may be different, for example, in the case of a provider serving a large number of customers).

Configuration directives – for example the Postfix directive reject_invalid_hostname – test the name announced by the server. Using conventional HELO tests results in a very high number of legitimate messages being rejected. However at the moment only few sites know how to modify HELO to make it work properly. This is probably going to change in the future since a growing number of sites will test HELO, thus creating an incentive to improve it.

Issues for consideration: These solutions may be considered when they concern the configuration.

Greylisting

This is the deliberate sending of an SMTP 4xx error code (a temporary error as opposed to a 5xx definitive error, see RFC 2821) when encountering a new sender. The latter, if it is a normal MTA, will try again later (usually 15 minutes later) and its message will then be accepted. Most spam software programs do not make multiple send attempts. This technique is highly effective and blocks all spam mails that are not sent through an open relay or by the MTA of a provider. It prevents receipt of certain messages from poorly configured servers and lends itself particularly well to be used in conjunction with a whitelist.

Issues for consideration: This technique is simple to implement but its future remains uncertain: if everybody adopts it, then spammers will start sending more messages again. Use of this could give techniques such as fingerprint filters time to show their merits before this method becomes less useful due to spammer adjustments.

Tokens/passwords

The aim of these techniques is to include a password in the address to which the e-mail is sent or to use a challenge/response system such as the Turing test. The spammer's software will not know this password and will be unable to pass the test.

These techniques have no false negatives – unless spammers decide to employ thousands of people at very low labour costs to do the work.

A certain number of legitimate users will refuse to or will be unable to pass the test. There will therefore be many false positives. These techniques are only of interest to highly popular recipients who already receive vast amounts of bulk mail, including legitimate mail, or to any recipient who wants to reduce the number of messages received, which falls within the scope of freedom of communication. It is necessary to be aware that not every sender will accept the test imposed. Educating users about the merits of this technology and taking the test may help reduce the non-acceptance rate.

Issues for consideration: These filters are not so much a filtering technique as part of a whitelisting policy. Users of such filters must be aware of this fact. Please refer to the above paragraph.

Various techniques

This section covers various techniques mostly experimental or insufficiently tested.

Envelope tests (BATV, SES)

These techniques are recent developments and insufficiently deployed to be taken into consideration.

Certification of Bulk Mails

Sender Reputation.

Although effective sender authentication will give Internet Service Providers (ISPs) a much more straightforward task when dealing with spam, authentication is only a preliminary step toward eliminating spam. Once the sender can be identified, factors such as reputation and accreditation are needed to determine whether a message should be classified as spam before it reaches the user. Independent authorities would manage the certification process and set the criteria. An oversight board, with cross-sector representation, would oversee the certification authorities.

Toward this end, the Trusted Email Open Standard (TEOS) has been created by the ePrivacy Group. TEOS grew out of ePrivacy's industry self-regulation program that aims to separate legitimate e-mail from spam. TEOS goes beyond authentication and creates a trusted identity for e-mail senders based on signatures in e-mail headers. Unlike the authentication signatures of DKIM, the TEOS signatures are visible seals in messages, certifying that the sender meets specified criteria.

There are a number of other organizations that are developing sender reputation schemes. Both America Online (AOL) and EarthLink use SPF to verify their outgoing e-mail. Brightmail and Microsoft will be using Brightmail's model to conduct joint testing on the efficacy of sender reputation systems. Further, Sendmail, a provider of secure e-mail systems, will be collaborating with Yahoo! to test DKIM.

Issues for consideration:	Unlike the authentication service, which is more empirically based, reputation and other services may have a larger subjective component provided by the rules/practices of the supplier. How their services will work and the credibility/utility of any particular service offering will have to be proven over time.

In order to reduce the problem of bulk e-mails erroneously filtered as spam, industry continues to discuss the efficacy of a bulk mail certification mechanism. For example, legitimate bulk mails could be identified at the ISP level with a label that is recognised by the server, thus enabling more confident use of e-mail filters. Several criteria could be used as input to the certification process, such as a commitment to strong privacy practices. For instance, France is working with its data protection agency (CNIL) towards a certification for senders who notify the use of client records.

Each ISP would maintain a whitelist of the certified clients. The proposal requires an agreement among ISPs on the certification process and involves no external intervention. However, the method would require a critical mass of ISP participation to be effective and would be based on trust among ISPs, since there is no external oversight of the certification process. In addition, assigning a fixed number to the definition of bulk mail may be problematic. Crafty spammers could use multiple free e-mail accounts to send large quantities of spam, with each account sending a number just under the pre-defined bulk mail threshold.

Micro payment systems

Conceptually, the simplest solution to the spam problem is requiring payment for each e-mail message that is sent, just as with conventional mail. Such a solution could be accomplished through structural changes to SMTP and would create a system in which a message was guaranteed to be delivered instead of suffering an ISP rejection on non-standard suspicion of spam. Money is the most obvious currency that could be used for payment but other ideas have been proposed.

For example, Microsoft has advocated computational spam-fighting, whereby each sent e-mail is paid for not in money but in computational time. Microsoft has proposed increasing the computational time to send each message to about ten seconds for unsolicited e-mail. This plan would have little effect on the casual e-mail sender, but those sending millions of messages a day would have to invest heavily into additional computational resources, a significant deterrent to sending spam. With this approach, users may choose to keep a whitelist, meaning that the list members would be exempt from the computational fee.

Another example is IronPort, whose Bonded Sender program is a whitelist certification program that requires a bulk e-mailer to post a monetary bond to gain accreditation. If the sender violates the acceptable e-mail practices, a debt is taken from the bond. Bonds range from USD 500 to more than USD 4 000, depending on monthly mail volume. Infractions, and bond debits, are based on user complaints. Microsoft has partnered with IronPort and will use the Bonded Sender program for incoming mail to its MSN and Hotmail accounts.

Does the sender's server reply if you try to respond?

There are no particular recommendations about using this technique.

PGP signatures

This technique is far too uncommon at present to be taken into consideration.

System configuration

Industrial and individual-level security best practices for ports, firewalls, networks, routers, proxies, access, passwords, permissions key protection and software installation are examples of use of system configuration as anti-spam technology. By configuring your system to block unwanted mail, one only captures some percentage of spam is captured. However, as more and more systems install these mechanisms, spammers will certainly become more ingenious, but it will also become less and less desirable to spam as there will be more obstacles to overcome. People spam now because it is simple, quick and cheap. As that changes – and hundreds of thousands of system administrators are working to change that situation – it will be harder to spam successfully.

Anti-virus tools

Anti-virus tools are important technologies that reduce the risk of spam e-mails infecting computer systems. Generally, harmful spam e-mails have potentially virus-initiating files attached. Anti-virus software can scan mailboxes and prevent virus infections.

Some ISPs are working to constantly monitor and update anti-virus API (application programming interface), VSAPI, with Exchange Server. This technology provides anti-virus scanning on user mailboxes to put scanning out to the network edge reducing the impact of viruses and virus-tainted e-mail on network infrastructures. It is also possible to prevent infected e-mail from leaving an organisation by scanning outgoing mail, in addition to incoming mail. The Clam Antivirus system http://www.clamav.net/ is an example of free software doing that same job.

Anti-spyware tools

Spyware has emerged as a major threat to enterprises because of the covert way it is installed to gather user information and deliver pop-up advertising. Spyware programs and keystroke loggers also have been used by malicious hackers to hijack e-mail addresses, user passwords and credit card information. Overall, spyware slows down computers, hijacks Web browsers, and sends personal information to advertisers. Anti-spyware tools can also detect potentially harmful spam e-mails, which in turn can assist the reduction of spam e-mail.

How to use this review of technologies and factors to consider

The utility of any tool(s) will be dependent on the needs, technical ability and the infrastructure of the user of the same tool. Tools are meant to be deployed at different parts across the system and for differing purposes. Users will have to consider their needs and strategies of defence in depth as they choose and deploy anti-spam tools. Tools themselves vary in maturity, efficacy, reliability and deployment. Some tools are more prone to false positives some are more effective in certain areas and some have greater overhead in terms of cost, infrastructure, bandwidth/capacity and needed technical expertise. A number of these factors have been listed for consideration, but user will have to gauge tools in the specific context of their contemplated application.

Some of the above tests are designed to fight spam, while others aim to prevent certain types of behaviour which pose a threat to security and fail to respect the resources of the platform to which mail is sent or simply do not comply with the accepted rules for sending electronic messages. When the rule is implemented after the receipt of the data constituting the message to be delivered, it remains to be decided how the message should be dealt with. This will obviously depend upon the results of the tests carried out. Some tests are more reliable than others and can therefore justify recourse to more drastic measures. Furthermore, it may be decided to carry out other and more expensive tests on certain messages.

The various options for dealing with a message depending on the location of the rule implemented are presented below.

Rejection in the SMTP session

The interest in such rejection lies in not taking charge of the electronic message, whose distribution remains the responsibility of the remote server, which has been advised of the situation. In addition it saves bandwidth capacity, firstly because the message is not received and secondly because the remote server will not have to send DSNs (Delivery Status Notification, the message generated in response to a rejection, see RFC 3461) that the message might generate. The task of issuing such a non-delivery message is transferred to the sender.

However, this type of rejection means that it is not possible to keep a copy of the message (and therefore to retrieve a legitimate message that might not have been accepted or simply to investigate a rejection).

Moreover, not all SMTP servers are currently able to run certain tests during the SMTP session. This is changing, however, with the increasingly common use of new products and in particular interfaces such as sendmail's "milter", the Postfix "policy server" or the future OPES which will be able to connect any program to the SMPT session.

Issues for consideration: Such rejection is advised.

Silent rejection

This method often confounds regular users who expect their e-mail to be delivered or at least to be told that it has been rejected. The "deliver or advise" alternative is a cardinal principle of e-mailing, but one which will probably have to be abandoned due to the number of "joejobs".[76]

Ideally, a record should be kept of e-mails destroyed in this way so that techniques such as Message Tracking can be used, for example by deploying RFC 3885 describing the message tracking protocol, which allows users to learn what happened with their messages (like the parcel tracking systems of typical parcel delivery companies).

Issues for consideration:	It should be noted that all "message losses" of the type complained about by users are not necessarily silent rejections by a provider. The cause of the loss may lie elsewhere (premature deletion of a message by the human recipient or deletion of a DSN by the human sender).

Rejection by sending a DSN (Delivery Status Notification or "bouncing")

This is the method traditionally used in Internet e-mailing. However, due to the presence of "joejobs", there is a risk of penalising innocent senders, as may be seen with the anti-virus programs which mistakenly send DSNs.

Issues for consideration:	If a message has been classified as spam, its sender's address is probably false and there is therefore no point in sending a DSN. Conversely, some server managers do not want to run the risk of failing to inform the sender that the message has not been distributed. It is difficult to recommend what approach to adopt in view of the advantages and disadvantages of each of these solutions.

Delivery to a spam box

When few messages are blocked on entry to the platform, the spam box can contain very large volumes of messages, which can discourage users from reading it. The message is not destroyed, but the user is given an opportunity to remedy false positives.

Issues for consideration:	This is a very useful complement to blocking on entry to the platform. The user can implement this technique to supplement the measures taken by his e-mailing provider if the latter does not offer a spam box in its anti-spam package.

Marking

The server takes no decision but simply places a note on the e-mail. This technique gives the user full control, but will also force the user to download spam mail.

Note that an e-mail service provider can offer the user the choice of simply marking the e-mail or delivering it to the spam box. It is relatively simple to manage.

Issues for consideration:	Marking the e-mail which modifies the message text or the Subject field is hazardous from both a technical standpoint (because it breaks signatures) and a legal one. It is preferable to add a header (such as "X-Provider-spamscanner: YES") that all e-mail software programs know how to use to filter mail.

This section contains discussions of the various anti-spam technologies and their capabilities presently available, as well as of the methods to be employed when spam is received. Any attempt to combat spam effectively must involve the sensible administration of a number of these technologies in concert. None of the above methods will be entirely successful in isolation. When a number of anti-spam technologies are effectively used in collaboration with one another, the effect can to drastically reduce the level of spam impacting a system.

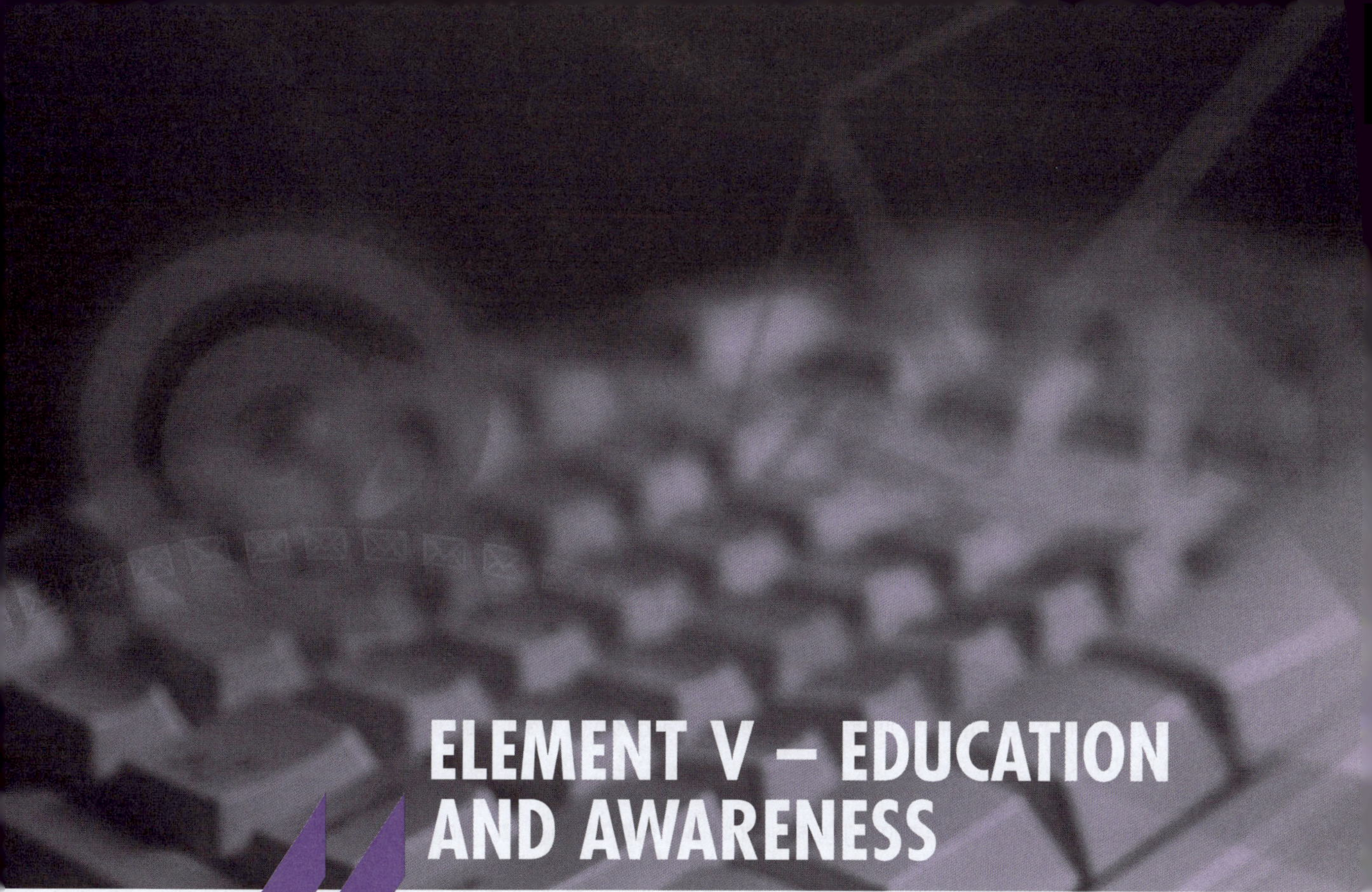

ELEMENT V – EDUCATION AND AWARENESS

Introduction

Governments, Internet service providers, marketing associations and other online operators can contribute to countering spam, establishing the appropriate legislative framework, ensuring effective law enforcement, implementing technical solutions and supporting co-operative approaches. Nevertheless a comprehensive anti-spam strategy must take into account the end-user, who is the final recipient of spam, the possible victim of viruses and scams and, at the same time, the person who has control over their computer and personal information.[77]

Considering that even a very low rate of response to spam allows spammers to make a profit from their activity,[78] increasing education and awareness is an important part of a comprehensive anti-spam strategy as it helps in reducing the potential "market" for spammers and consequently their financial incentives to continue spamming.

Notwithstanding the large amount of readily available information and material, and the widespread opinion that spam is bad and potentially harmful, it is clear that some recipients are still opening spam messages, clicking on advertised links, or even purchasing the product offered. In addition, in response to increasingly sophisticated phishing techniques, users are still tricked into disclosing personal information and passwords.[79]

For the above reasons it is apparent that education and awareness-raising activities are still needed, and may need to be reinforced, to change users' behaviour vis-à-vis spam and other online security threats. It seems that security is not yet perceived as a real issue, and most users are not aware of the risks connected to online chatting, e-mailing, gaming and surfing. A culture of security should be developed, as a responsible use of cyberspace is at the basis of the development of the digital economy.

Education and awareness strategies: targeting the audience

Education and awareness activities should target users first and foremost, but also large corporations, small and medium-sized enterprises, direct marketers and online operators. All of these stakeholders are actively involved in the information society, and contribute to online activities. In this context, the OECD anti-spam Toolkit aims to contribute to the creation of a culture of security by developing an online repository for educational resources, and awareness8raising material which has been developed in a number of countries using a number of different languages. The objective is to make these tools available to other private or public bodies that are willing to undertake similar initiatives, and which would benefit from available material. This will help in minimising duplication of effort and support the development of a more comprehensive and uniform approach, promoting best practices and highlighting success stories. This resource will be particularly useful for developing economies that have very limited resources to devote to spam.

The OECD Spam Toolkit page relating to education will contain links and materials organised depending on the target of the specific initiative: individual users; children and students; corporate users; and e-mail marketing companies and associations. Under each title there will be the link to resources and materials and the indication of the language. The Netherlands Ministry of Economic Affairs has prepared the brochure "Sp@m: *do's and don'ts*" and provided this to the Task Force, so that it can be posted in electronic format on the OECD Toolkit website at www.oecd-antispam.org, and can be used by any entity wishing to distribute or make available information and tips for users on how to deal with spam. The brochure is available in English and French, but with contributions from the task force members it would be possible to provide it in other languages.

Individual users

The entities best placed to reach individual users on the Web are ISPs and ESPs. Through their Web pages they can provide information on how to avoid spam, anti-spam and anti-virus filters and why it is important to use them, as well as guidance on how to report spam abuses to the authorities. In addition, through acceptable use policies endorsed by the client in a subscription contract, the provider is able to set a series of rules forbidding the use of their service to send spam, viruses or other illegal content.

General awareness activities can be posted on the Web or other media such as television, newspapers and magazines. Brochures can be distributed in schools, made available on ISPs website, and also distributed as a leaflet in IT magazines. Educational cartoons about spam and online security have been broadcast in some European countries. Well-known comics have been used to promote safe Internet browsing for children.

The messages sent to users need to be clear and harmonised. For example in Canada the campaign "Stop Spam Here"[80] emphasised "Three Key Tips": protect your computer, protect your e-mail address, protect yourself. Under these three elements advice was provided to users. Australia launched the catchy slogan "Don't try, don't buy, don't reply to spam"[81] which, while it does not substitute for appropriate education on issues, helps raise awareness on some basic tips to avoid being spammed.

In addition, national-wide campaigns can also have a positive impact, by getting the attention of the population and of the media. On 7 February 2006 a total of 37 countries, and around 100 organisations, took part in the *Safer Internet Day*, which was organised across Europe and worldwide under the auspices of the European Commission[82]. In the United States, the FTC, the Department of Homeland Security, the Department of Commerce, and other government and private sector partners have launched a Web site and education campaign to help individuals be on guard about Internet fraud. The campaign is called OnGuard Online, and is available at: http://www.OnGuardOnline.gov in both English and Spanish. It uses straightforward, plain-language materials to help computer users be on guard against Internet fraud, secure their computers, and protect their personal information. The materials on OnGuard Online are available to anyone who is interested in using them and interested parties are encouraged to consider partnering with the Web site. The ICPEN, the International Consumer Protection and Enforcement Network, has launched a yearly fraud prevention campaign. One of the main themes dealt with during the February 2006 campaign was spam.

User groups

User groups can be targeted with information tailored to their needs. These may include:

- **Senior citizens**: computer classes for seniors are the best place to introduce the concept of computer and information security, and teach these new users how to deal with spam, avoid viruses and recognise scams.

- **Children and students**: awareness of online threats and security issues should be part of their educational curriculum. Schools should include in their computer courses sessions regarding spam, online frauds and viruses, illegal content, and netiquette. Also, parents play a big role in teaching children how to be safe online, making them understanding the risks of online communications, and how to protect themselves (See Box 4).

Box 4. Children education

Several educational initiatives use cartoon characters and interactive games to teach children how to behave safely while online. In particular, children are taught not to open or reply to e-mails coming from unknown senders, not to disclose personal information on line, and to report to their parents every time they receive or otherwise see online information that makes them uncomfortable.

Source: http://www.cnil.fr; http://www.saftonline.org/Education/; http://disney.go.com/surfswell/index.html.

Users and phishing

Phishing is a complex phenomenon, which includes social as well as technological factors. For this reason a solution implies: the implementation of technical measures to limit the phenomenon and reduce the consequent damages; the effort of online operators to establish, implement, and enforce appropriate and clear policies on e-mail practices with their customers (see Element III, industry-driven solutions); and the development of consumer education initiatives.

Awareness campaigns are essential to educate individuals on how to recognise and respond to deceptive and fraudulent messages. Government authorities, online operators and ISPs are currently developing educational tools for users.[83] Also in this case, to be effective, the message transmitted to users needs to be simple and unified, at the same time touching the user emotionally and calling for action. Some of the provisions which should be stressed include:

- Instruct users receiving an e-mail asking for personal information to call the company directly to **ask for confirmation** or type in the company's correct Web address, while **avoiding clicking on the link provided in the e-mail**.

- Advise users to **utilise antivirus software and firewalls** to protect their computer and avoid accepting unwanted files that could harm a computer or track a consumer's Internet activities.

- Warn users against e-mailing personal or financial information.

Companies and small medium-sized enterprises

Companies are often the victims of spam and malware, as their e-mail addresses are posted on public Web sites or widely circulated, and they usually have always-on broadband connections. It may be necessary to make a distinction between larger companies, and small and medium-sized enterprises, since the latter often cannot afford sufficient internal technical support or company-wide policies and procedures for computer security, but have to rely on the scrupulousness of their employees. Educational needs are therefore different:

- **Large companies**: the administration should make available to new staff: a pamphlet explaining the company's security policy for e-mail, existing filters, and best practices for dealing with spam (don't open, don't click, etc.). The same kind of information should be available on the internal Web site, and updates can be sent to users periodically by e-mail (see Box 4).

- **SMEs**: they should be provided with specific information on simplified security management practices, training material, software, etc. In this case the entities in the best position to help would include the ISPs and the security software companies, but also associations (such as the chambers of commerce and artisan associations) which could contribute in raising awareness of the problem among their members and point to possible solutions.

Box 5. Security tips and tricks: An example of a company's anti-spam internal policy[84]

Protect your e-mail address:

- Try not to display your e-mail address in public. This includes on Web sites, newsgroup postings or in an online service's membership directory.
- Where a public e-mail address is required, you can request the IT department to create a generic account, e.g. spam.project@oecd.org
- Consider masking your e-mail address. It is simple to add a space just before and after the @ (for example joedoe @ myisp.com). this might prevent harvesting machines and other automatic spamming technologies from recognizing your address. It may however not be advisable to use this system if you need to receive confirmation of a service, for example.
- Decide if you want to use one or more e-mail addresses – one for professional messages, another for newsgroups and directories, etc. Alternative free e-mail addresses can be obtained at most major ISPs.
- Check the Privacy Policy when you submit your address to a Web site. See if it allows the company to sell your address or for which kind of promotional activities it can be used.
- Read and understand the entire form before you transmit personal information through a Web site. Often there are pre-selected boxes saying you agree to receive e-mail from the company's "partners". You should uncheck the box to opt out.
- Remember that by law, you should be able to unsubscribe to unwanted messages by "opting-out".

Protect your computer:

Do not forget that a spam message may contain more than just a special offer on Viagra. It could also contain a virus, so be extremely careful if you decide to open the message. Should you receive a suspicious e-mail, the best thing to do is to delete the entire message, including any attachments. Then delete it from your deleted items folder. If you have to open an attachment, then the following procedure is suggested:

- Be sure your virus software is up to date
- Save the file to your hard disk
- Scan the file using your anti-virus software
- If no viruses were detected, open the file

It is also a good idea not to reply to unsolicited messages. Hackers and spammers sometimes look for a response to confirm an e-mail address is active, before they add an unwitting user to a distribution list. This practice however can be difficult to apply in countries adopting an opt-out system, where senders can send messages without the previous consent of the user, who however always has the possibility to unsubscribe.

Box 5. Security tips and tricks: An example of a company's anti-spam internal policy (cont'd)

You can use free anti-spam software filters, such as SpamAssassin or others, to automatically move spam messages to a "junk mail" file.

Protect your data:

- Use secure passwords, change them frequently and do not disclose them over unsecured communication mechanisms, such as e-mail.

Also additional mechanisms may consist in:

- "Lock the door when you leave the house" – Turn off the computer and disconnect from the network if you are not using it.
- Do not run programmes of unknown origins. Despite their qualifications, they may install spyware and other malware on your computer, and even transform it into a remotely run zombie drone.
- Report serious incidents.
- Help other people in your company to protect their e-mail, computer, and the network.

The education of recipients is as important as the education of senders. In this context, companies using e-mails to communicate with their clients should also receive information on how to appropriately use this communication medium without being considered spammers and be sanctioned as part of national anti-spam legislation. Simple mailing practices should be respected by all entities.

In addition, companies should control more closely the quality of their affiliates and subcontractors, especially for outsourced advertising contracts.

Direct marketing companies

Specific attention should be paid to spam legislation by direct marketers. They need to know and carefully observe anti-spam legislation in force in the country of origin and in the country of destination of the message. To help their members in complying with the legislation, direct marketing associations are providing lists of online marketing best practices, often in the form of a "check-list" indicating the requirements a company must fulfil from the moment it decides to launch an online advertisement campaign to the actual sending of the message. The check-list contains references to the applicable provisions, indication on how to lawfully collect and use e-mail addresses, and specific information and wording which need to be included in the text of the message (for example the unsubscribe option, or the mailing address of the company), as well as suggestions to avoid being inadvertently filtered out as spam. In this context, the Task Force encouraged the adoption of a set of best practices for e-mail marketing by private-sector representatives, which are currently being developed by BIAC members (see Element III).

ELEMENT VI – CO-OPERATIVE PARTNERSHIPS AGAINST SPAM

The liberalisation of the telecommunication market, together with the growth of the Internet, driven by private players and being largely unregulated, contributed to the shaping of the actual information society, in which all stakeholders – governments, private companies, civil society and users – have a role to play and can contribute to its development.

Issues such as spam and cybersecurity are affecting public and private players, and therefore there is a common interest in preserving the availability and reliability of communication tools to promote the development of the digital economy. While the objective is shared, there could be conflict in the way it is achieved. Governments follow public policy objectives, and their involvement is essential to set far-reaching goals and elaborate a comprehensive anti-spam strategy. However, legislative instruments alone are not always effective and their mechanisms can be too rigid to address the rapidly evolving spam (and malware) landscape. Industry players are well placed to undertake concrete and timely actions. Although it is a business reality that some activities cannot be justified from a competitive business perspective, certain incentives would help to ensure that companies align themselves with the interests of the wider community.

There are different approaches which could be used to fill this gap, from a government-led regulatory approach, whereby the regulator sets the rules, imposing certain responsibilities on private companies, such as for example the obligation to apply security practices, to the more market-led approach where private operators autonomously decide their level of involvement and participation. In the middle there are a variety of possibilities, which include the approaches undertaken by several OECD governments, focusing on the establishment of appropriate regulatory and enforcement frameworks, and using general policy tools to encourage industry participation.

The public and private sectors have found a number of diverse and innovative ways to co-operate: governments seek the involvement of private sector entities, as well as non-governmental bodies, in the discussion of comprehensive anti-spam strategies and activities. The objectives of strategic partnerships are usually to improve networking, awareness raising activities and information sharing. More operational partnerships also contribute to education, development (and application) of best practices and exchange of information and data on cross-border spam cases. In addition, as the various efforts taking place at national and international levels shows, partnerships are a fundamental tool to improve communication, understanding of reciprocal needs, expectations and problems, and therefore allow further co-operation and mutual involvement.

Examples of public-private partnerships currently dealing with the problem of spam include, for example, the Australian ACMA, which worked with the Internet Industry Association (IIA) in order to develop codes of conduct for ISPs and online direct marketers.[85] The Canadian Task Force on Spam included representatives from private and public sectors, civil society and academia,[86] who jointly contributed to the elaboration of a series of recommendations and best practices to fight spam. France, with its project "Signal Spam"[87] put together public authorities and private players to develop a system to simplify the signalling of spam by users and standardise spam processing and analysis in order to improve efficiency and co-ordination of anti-spam actions.[88] At EU level, the "SpotSpam" initiative funded under the EU Safer Internet Plus Programme aims to facilitate evidence gathering and exchange of information where legal action is taken against a spammer, and to provide a supranational source of information to monitor spam complaints.[89]

On the operational side, the London Action Plan (LAP),[90] created in October 2004, is currently particularly active and counts an increasing number of participants from public and private sectors. The activities of the LAP include regular (tri-monthly) conference calls among the different members to discuss new initiatives against spam, share information and best practices, as well as one-time initiatives on a specific subject, as for example the "spam sweep day", which involved authorities from different countries, and the "zombies project"[91], recently launched (see Element III: industry-driven initiatives). One of the objectives of the group is to facilitate contact between enforcement agencies, promote information exchange in cross-border actions, and increase the co-operation with ISPs and other private operators.

Private-public partnerships in the field of spam are necessary to promote interaction and co-operation between the two players, especially considering the wide array of stakeholders involved and their different needs and backgrounds. Relying only on legislation to impose obligations on private players would not be effective unless combined with other measures. As an example, laws cannot keep up with technical change. Best-practices, if widely applied, can be effective combined with legal and other measures. In this context, strategic partnerships, such as those taking place with the different task forces created at national and international levels, are a fundamental tool to improve communication, understanding of reciprocal needs, expectations and problems, and therefore allow further co-operation and mutual involvement.

For the partnership to be successful and achieve concrete results, which will then be put into practice by the different stakeholders, it seems therefore that the following elements[92] are necessary:

- Commitment and real contribution of all parties; ownership of the end product.
- A well-defined objective and timeframe.
- One (or more) leaders, who put more resources and effort into the project.

- National partnerships that feed into international initiatives and partnerships, to complement and harmonise solutions.

- Rather than duplicating effort, when possible, partnerships should build on existing trusted relationships and representative bodies.

The OECD Spam Task Force is in itself a co-operative partnership, bringing together representatives from different sectors and a large number of countries. The Task Force set its objectives, which are strategic, involving the creation of an information network between different players, but also operational, as the group aims at the production of a policy Toolkit which should help the definition of comprehensive anti-spam strategies at the national and international levels. At the same time, however, the involvement of the private sector needs to be increased and widened, and governmental players should develop a sense of ownership of the result of this work, which will constitute an important message to all stakeholders, in OECD as well as non-OECD economies, on the necessity to combat spam and malware, the best applicable solutions, and the effort put into this endeavour by OECD players.[93]

The OECD Council Recommendation on Spam Cross-Border Enforcement Co-operation specifically encourage governments to cooperate with businesses, industry groups and consumer groups in the pursuit of spammers, user education, referral of relevant complaint data, and to share investigation tools and techniques, analysis and data. Public-private co-operation is also considered crucial in international efforts, in order to efficiently enforce the legislation, reduce the incidence of inaccurate information about holders of domain names,[94] and overall to make the Internet more secure.

The Task Force also encouraged the development of best common practices for e-mail marketing and for ISPs. Best practices were elaborated by a cross-sectoral group of private players, and are attached as annexes to this report (Annexes II and III). Last but not least, measurement of spam is an important instrument which could be developed only with the intervention of private sector operator, but that would assist policy makers and authorities to evaluate the impact of their regulatory initiatives and enforcement efforts. In the framework of the Task Force work, the MAAWG developed the Email Metrics Program, which is mentioned in Element VII below.

Public-private sector co-operation is an element which underlies multiple anti-spam activities and initiatives, therefore the different initiatives have been dealt with in more detail in the relevant elements of this Report.

ELEMENT VII – SPAM MEASUREMENT

Spam metrics

At the beginning of this report it was noted that spam is evolving. Although there are many different sources providing data on the amount of e-mail categorised as spam, the percentage of viruses and the number of phishing scams sent through electronic messages, the information is not easily comparable, and diverging results are reported. This is due to lack of a common international definition of spam, and to the different methodologies used to measure the amount of spam, which depend on the various filtering technologies employed.

Most of the data on spam originates from industry, in particular from anti-spam solution providers, but also by Internet Service Providers (although the latter data are not usually available to the public). Data gathered by these players are difficult to compare as they relate to a different user base and are founded on different parameters. This raises a number of questions about the completeness of data, what is being measured, and if industry should be encouraged to develop a single methodology for data collection. In addition, Internet Service Providers are often unwilling to disclose information which is sensitive for the company and may damage their competitiveness.

Filtering companies and ISPs (using filters) collect data from their customers that provide measures on the amount of spam detected by the filters. These data provide an indication of the growth of spam relative to the total volume of e-mail, the different possible content, and the affected countries. Anti-spam organisations and bodies related to consumer or privacy protection also measure spam. In addition, but to a limited extent, data on spam are collected by some governmental or public organisations which have the responsibility to develop anti-spam policies or regulations.

Statistics prepared by anti-spam solution providers show that in 2005 the average percentage of spam e-mails decreased slightly, reaching 68.6% of total e-mail, compared to 72.3% in 2004.[95] AOL declared that already between 2003 and 2004 the number of spam messages blocked by their filters had declined by half, and so did the number of spam complaints from their customers. Different sources noted that spam is affecting users to a lesser extent, often thanks to the utilization of spam filters and anti-virus protection, and to educational and awareness campaigns, which teach users how to deal with the phenomenon. The change in the spam trend, which had been growing in previous years, demonstrates that the implementation of appropriate technical solutions, coupled with an aggressive approach to spammers (legal suits, investigations), can bring results. Rresearch from the Finnish Statistics Institute concluded that households in Finland are generally moderately concerned about spam. Similarly, according to research of the Pew Internet and American Life Project, 22% of users say they spend less time on e-mail because of spam, down from the 29 per cent in 2004.[96]

Statistics can also provide relevant information to policy makers with respect to burdens that spam imposes on network operators. For example, according to VeriSign, the manager of the .com and .net domains, during the three-month period from 1 July to 20 September, 2004, spam represented 80% of traffic by volume, but constituted only 21 percent of e-mail bandwidth because the average size of a spam message was 3K bytes, while the average size of a legitimate message was 40K bytes.[97] Thus, while spam clearly creates considerable costs for operators of e-mail servers, the volume of spam does not appear to be destabilising the e-mail system.

Measurement is key to evaluating the evolution of spam and the effectiveness of anti-spam solutions and educational efforts, to be able to determine if a strategy is effective, and eventually what changes are needed in policy, regulatory and technical frameworks.

In order to better assess the current status of spam, and provide data on the amount of spam which passes in the network, the Messaging Anti-Abuse Working Group (MAAWG), in the context of the Task Force work, developed an E-mail Metrics Program and agreed on a series of ISPs spam indicators to measure:[98]

- The total number of dropped connections resulting from IP blocking (while this parameter may be imprecise, it gives a sense of the magnitude of the amount of messages which are not penetrating the networks).
- The total number of blocked or tagged inbound e-mails and percentage of e-mails going through the ISPs (excluding blocked connections) that are identified as spam.
- The focus is therefore on "unwanted" e-mail, so that the difficulty of defining spam will be avoided.

For the last quarter of 2005, the total number of inbound emails filtered is about 203 billion. Of these, the delivery of more than 61 billion has been refused using RBLs (Real Time Blacklists) or other methods, while another 142 billion have been successively blocked or tagged using ASAV (Anti-Spam/Anti-Viral) framework, MTAs (Mail Transfer Agents) and other recipient- or message-based rules. This does not include additional filtering at the MUAs (Mail User Agents) level.

This means that for the last quarter of 2005 there have been:

- Approximately 500 dropped connections per mailbox.
- More than 1.5 dropped connections per unaltered delivered e-mail.

- More than 1 000 blocked/tagged inbound e-mails per mailbox.
- Approximately 4 blocked/tagged inbound e-mails per unaltered delivered e-mail or 80% of total number of inbound messages.

If we factor in 1 abusive e-mail per dropped connection, the ratio of blocked/tagged inbound e-mails per unaltered delivered e-mail increases to 5.6 emails or 85% of inbound messages (see Figure 2).

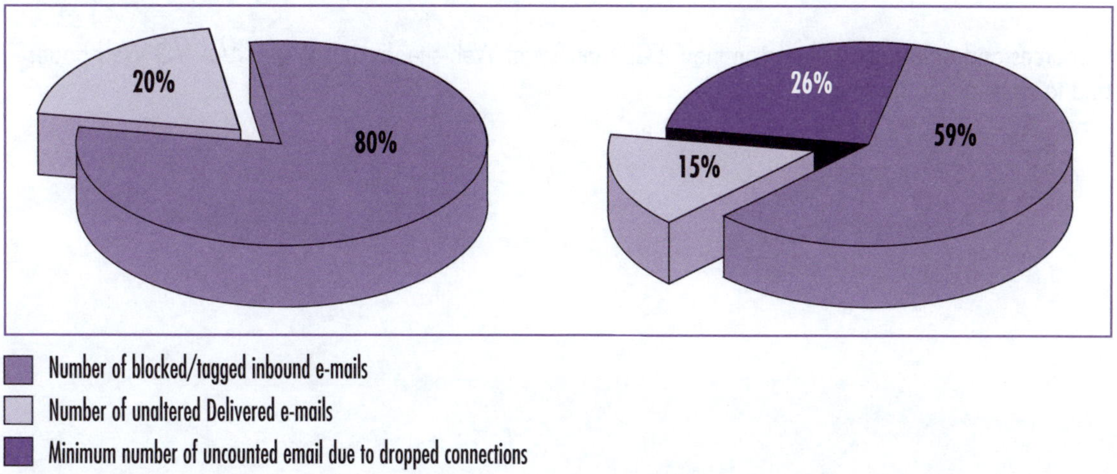

Source: MAAWG Email Metrics Program, March 2006.

Figure 2. Percentage of spam e-mails at ISPs level (4Q2005)

The report will be updated on a quarterly basis in an attempt to identify trends over time. Mailbox operators voluntarily decided to participate and commit to supply confidential data for two years on a quarterly basis.[99] Data will be available on the MAAWG Web site (www.maawg.org), or on the OECD anti-spam pages at: www.oecd-antispam.org, under "Statistics".

ISPs' data can be compared with measurements of spam as it is perceived by the user, in their inbox **after** the application of filters and other technical solutions. In order to obtain a more detailed analysis of the spam phenomenon, France undertook a statistical study based on «inbox spam». The preliminary results of the study, based on public statistical rules, suitably complete the existing statistical information. The mentioned approach is different as it does not measure the spam "in the pipeline", but spam which reaches the end-user and is perceived by the latter as being spam. This type of measure provides a more sociological analysis of what users consider spam, and how concerned they are by the phenomenon.

Regarding the first issue, about 90% of interviewees consider spam any commercial e-mail from a sender they cannot identify or a commercial e-mail from a sender to whom they certainly did not give their e-mail address. In addition, 74% consider unsolicited (non-commercial) messages sent by political parties or trade unions as spam.

Notwithstanding most of the users can easily identify spam e-mails and eliminate them, still 8% of respondents affirmed they bought a good or service advertised in such a message. A large part of the interviewees are aware of the necessity to take precautions to avoid being spammed. In particular, protecting personal e-mail addresses and using anti-spam filter services are the most common procedures.

The second issue relates to how concerned people are about spam. The survey showed that while most users received a small amount of spam, and therefore were not very concerned with the problem, about 10% of users receive 70% of the total volume of spam, and consider it to be a major annoyance.

Resources and data are available on the OECD Anti-Spam Web site, linking to the MAAWG Web pages and to other online statistics.

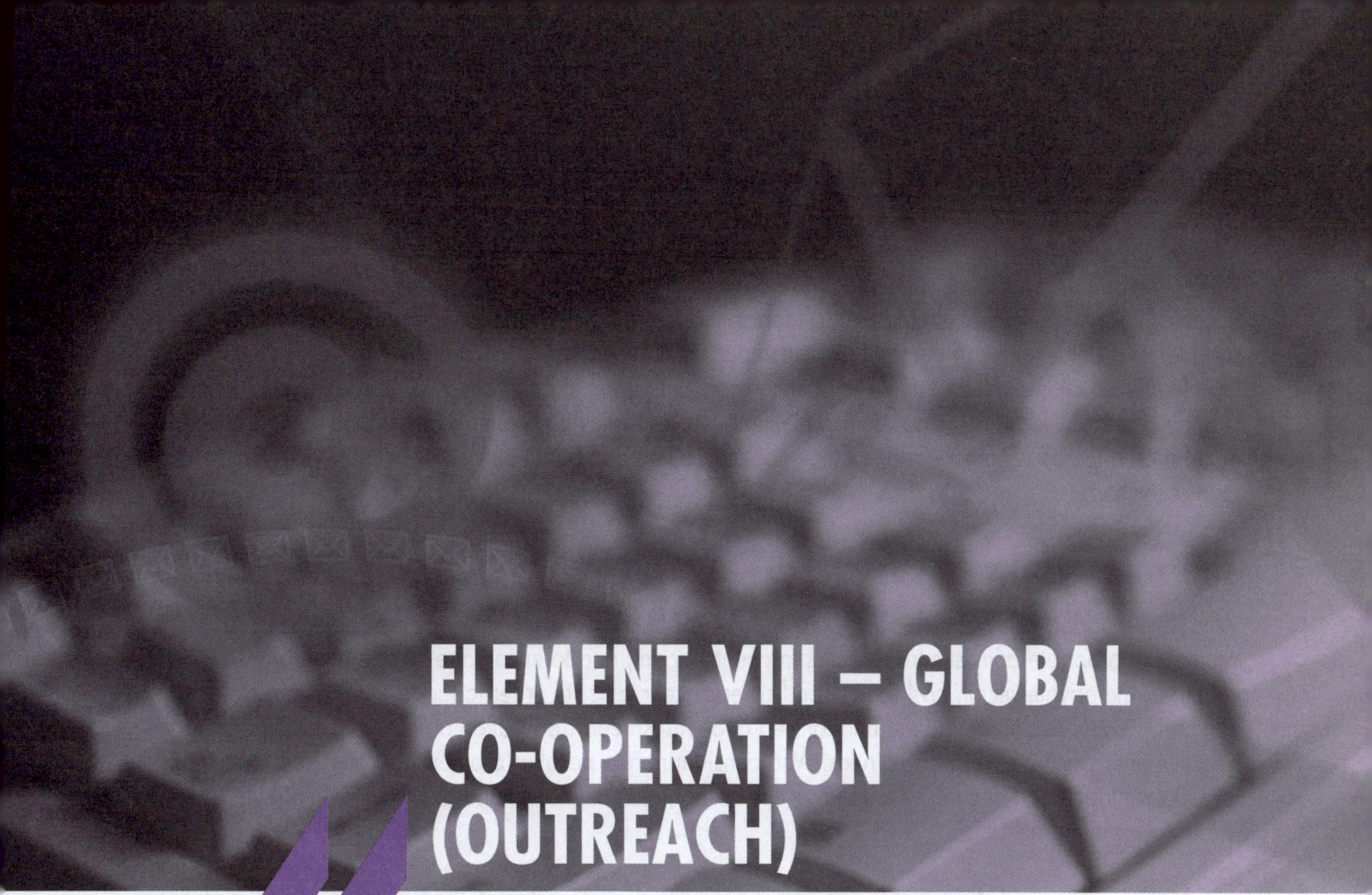

ELEMENT VIII – GLOBAL CO-OPERATION (OUTREACH)

Introduction

Spam is a concern for developing countries, as for developed ones, which are facing the same problems as their developed counterparts,[100] with, in addition, limitations due to the lack of technical, financial and knowledge resources. In particular:

- The available bandwidth is often lower.
- Most of the users connect through dial-up or in cyber cafes, therefore network connections are more expensive and slow, which also has implications for the financial impact of spam.
- ISPs are often not aware of the dangers connected to spam and viruses, or do not have the resources to fight them.

The application of technical solutions (filters, anti-virus software, etc.) may be difficult, as they are relatively expensive. In addition, the legislative framework may be incomplete, as the applicability of general consumer protection and data privacy laws to the Internet may be unclear. Even when some legislation is in place, there are not the necessary resources or authorities to enforce these laws against spammers.

Often spammers – for whom it has become difficult or too risky to operate from a developed country, or who are considered *"persona non grata"* by ISPs – may exploit the above-mentioned weaknesses to move their traffic to countries where they know they can operate more easily and enjoy a certain degree of impunity. In some cases this is also due to a lax anti-spam and security policy on the ISP side. Of course it is not an exclusive problem of developing countries (networks of zombie computers are also a reality in developed countries, as are the well-known "pink contracts" between ISPs and spammers), however its consequences can be particularly dangerous, especially considering that in many countries, such as India, where the IT infrastructure is relatively well developed, ISPs are often being exploited by spammers.

While in most cases ISPs are not even aware of what is going on on their network, in other cases they accept to take spammers in exchange for financial compensation. This tactic, which seems profitable in the short term, is catastrophic in the long term: complacent ISPs will get blacklisted by other providers, and their legitimate clients will be unable to communicate with users in other countries, and may decide to change providers. Blacklists, discussed in Element IV, are particularly criticised by providers and public authorities in the developing world, as they are seen as an additional burden on local population, rather than a solution.

The role of global co-operation (Outreach)

What is the added value of outreach in this area? Global co-operation has two main objectives: to promote appropriate domestic frameworks to counter spam; and to encourage co-operation among countries, the private sector, civil society and other stakeholders, in order to tackle the problem of spam comprehensively and to ensure the harmonised and widespread application of technical measures and the effective enforcement of applicable rules. Also considering the peculiar problems encountered in non-OECD countries when dealing with spam, it seems that international co-operation could contribute greatly, in particular in the field of:

- **Laws and regulation enforcement**: International co-operation in the field of law and regulation is fundamental, to support the establishment of an appropriate anti-spam regulatory framework in all countries – possibly following a set of basic principles harmonised at the international level. National policy should include facilitating international co-operation and the sharing of information and practices. In addition, enforcement actions undertaken in some countries have a global effect, benefiting users all over the world.

- **Education**: Educational and awareness tools which have already been developed should be made available more generally to all users, operators, schools and public authorities in all countries. Considering that in most developing economies Internet access is often "collective", i.e. users connect from work, school, or using one of the available community access points, such as cybercafés and public libraries, educational materials should be disseminated in these locations, thereby reaching a large number of users at the same time.

- **Facilitate industry co-operation**: The establishment of a series of best common practices is a global objective, and all ISPs should be involved. Practices suggested by various industry associations, public-private initiatives, or the suggestions included in this Report (see Best Practices for ISPs in Element III), could provide a good basis. The commitment of industry will be necessary for further steps. In particular, international co-operation would be useful to bring together ISPs from developed economies, which have considerable experience in the field, and their counterparts in developing economies, in order to share their knowledge, experiences and best practices.

OECD Outreach activities

Developing countries have, in several instances, called for more support from more technical-developed countries and the international community in facing the problem of spam, and more generally of Internet security. The creation of a framework for effective co-operation across borders is warmly supported from both sides. In this context, it seems that the work of the OECD Spam Task Force, and in particular the Anti-Spam Toolkit, could be a useful resource for all interested stakeholders.

To promote co-operation and information exchange and facilitate the dissemination of the Toolkit, the Task Force created a website (www.oecd-antispam.org) providing material on education, regulatory and technical measures, and a contact list of enforcement authorities and anti-spam legislation around the world. The website is updated thanks to the contributions of participating countries. Non-OECD economies are also welcome to send data and information on their national frameworks.

In addition, the OECD is taking part and contributing to anti-spam initiatives at the global level, in partnership with other organisations active in this field, such as the ITU, the EU and APEC.

CONCLUDING REMARKS

In order for electronic communications to contribute to economic and social development, they must be reliable, efficient and trustworthy. Today users' confidence in electronic communication tools, and in particular e-mail, may be threatened by unsolicited, unwanted, and harmful electronic messages, commonly known as spam.

The openness and decentralisation of the Internet are the main reasons for the medium's success. All the applications and services developed in the past years - peer to peer, Voice over IP – spread rapidly and without the need of any approval or formality. Anybody can decide how to employ or innovate the network. However, these characteristics also create a number of vulnerabilities that are increasingly exploited by spammers and other online offenders. The lack of centralised control enables users to hide their identity. In addition, the low cost of accessing Internet and e-mail services allows spammers to send out millions of spam messages every day. Therefore, it is necessary to combat spam and other threats, while simultaneously avoiding damage to the communications medium we are trying to protect.

The first question Task Force members had to answer, at the beginning of their mandate, was not whether members should or should not take action against spam, but the appropriate action to take. An important lesson which should be learnt is that the problem of spam is complex, and that a multi-stakeholder and multi-pronged approach is fundamental.

As became clear in the work of the Task Force, all stakeholders have an important role in fighting spam. Governments should work to establish clear national anti-spam policies in concert with other players, collaborate with private operators, and promote co-operation across borders. Setting up domestic co-ordination groups, and creating the appropriate regulatory frameworks – based on well-defined policy objectives – backed by effective enforcement mechanisms, can greatly contribute to the anti-spam battle.

On the basis of this framework, the private sector has the lead role for the development of relevant business practices and innovative technical solutions, and can greatly contribute to the education of users. Coordination and co-operation among public and private players is critical to achieve results in the fight against spam.

Considering the rapid pace of technical evolution, and therefore the changing of fraudulent and illicit online practices, this Toolkit is not trying to provide specific answers, but policy orientation. Also, the complexity of the problem will not change after the Task Force completes its mandate, whence the importance to establish and maintain a clear strategy to fight spam. Continuous national co-ordination and public-private co-operation and dialogue are instrumental in this endeavour.

The Internet is defined by the WSIS Declaration of Principles as "*a global facility available to the public*". This means it is also the responsibility of the entire public to preserve it and contribute to its usability and reliability. All players need to learn how to deal with spam. To this end, the toolkit-approach needs to be implemented at the national level, and should be reviewed regularly in order to address new threats and illegal activities for which spam is the vehicle.

ANNEXES

Annex I: Recommendation of the Council on Cross-Border Co-operation in the Enforcement of Laws Against Spam

THE COUNCIL,

Having regard to the Convention on the Organisation for Economic Co-operation and Development of 14th December 1960, in particular Article 5 (b) thereof;

Recognising that spam undermines consumer confidence, which is a prerequisite for the information society and for the success of e-commerce;

Recognising that spam can facilitate the spread of viruses, serve as the vehicle for traditional fraud and deception as well as for other Internet-related threats such as phishing, and that its effects can negatively impact the growth of the digital economy, thus resulting in important economic and social costs for Member countries and non-member economies;

Recognising that spam poses unique challenges for law enforcement in that senders can easily hide their identity, forge the electronic path of their email messages, and send their messages from anywhere in the world to anyone in the world, thus making spam a uniquely international problem that can only be efficiently addressed through international co-operation;

Recognising the need for global co-operation to overcome a number of challenges to information gathering and sharing, for identifying enforcement priorities and for developing effective international enforcement frameworks;

Recognising that current measures, such as numerous bi- and multilateral criminal law enforcement co-operation instruments, provide a framework for enforcement co-operation on criminal conduct associated with spam, such as malware and phishing;

Having regard to the *Recommendation of the Council concerning Guidelines for Protecting Consumers from Fraudulent and Deceptive Commercial Practices Across Borders* (hereinafter "*Cross-border Fraud Guidelines*"), which sets forth principles for international co-operation among consumer protection enforcement agencies in combating cross-border fraud and deception [C(2003)116];

Having regard to the *Recommendation of the Council concerning Guidelines Governing the Protection of Privacy and Transborder Flows of Personal Data* [C(80)58] (hereinafter "*Privacy Guidelines*"), and the *Ministerial Declaration on the Protection of Privacy on Global Networks* [C(98)177];

Recognising that, in some instances, the *Cross-border Fraud Guidelines* and the *Privacy Guidelines* may apply directly to cross-border spam enforcement co-operation and that even where this is not the case, many of the principles expressed in these Guidelines can be usefully tailored to develop appropriate national frameworks and facilitate international co-operation to enforce laws against spam;

Recalling that, while cross-border enforcement co-operation is an important element in tackling the global problem of spam, it is necessary in this respect to adopt a comprehensive national approach which also addresses regulatory and policy issues, facilitates the development of appropriate technical solutions, improves education and awareness among all players and encourages industry-driven initiatives;

On the joint proposal of the Committee for Information, Computer and Communications Policy and the Committee on Consumer Policy:

AGREES that:

For the purposes of this Recommendation, and without prejudice to other existing co-operation instruments "Spam Enforcement Authorities" means any national public body, as determined by each Member country, that is responsible for enforcing Laws Connected with Spam and has powers to (a) co-ordinate or conduct investigations or (b) pursue enforcement proceedings, or (c) both.

For the purposes of this Recommendation, "Laws Connected with Spam" means (a) laws specifically targeting electronic communications; or (b) general laws, such as privacy laws, consumer protection laws or telecommunication laws that may apply to electronic communications.

This Recommendation is primarily aimed at national public bodies, with enforcement authority for Laws Connected with Spam. It is recognised that some Member countries have many competent bodies, some of which are regional or local, that can take or initiate action against spam. It is also recognised that, in some Member countries, private enforcement bodies may play a very important role in ensuring enforcement of Laws Connected with Spam, including in cross-border situations.

This Recommendation covers cross-border spam enforcement co-operation only in areas where the conduct prohibited by the Laws Connected with Spam of the Member country receiving a request for assistance is substantially similar to conduct prohibited by the Laws Connected with Spam of the Member country requesting assistance. Co-operation under this Recommendation does not affect the freedom of expression as protected in laws of Member countries.

Co-operation under this Recommendation focuses on those violations of Laws Connected with Spam that are most serious in nature, such as those that (a) cause or may cause injury (financial or otherwise) to a significant number of recipients, (b) affect particularly large numbers of recipients (c) cause substantial harm to recipients.

In all instances, the decision on whether to provide assistance under this Recommendation rests with the Spam Enforcement Authority receiving the request for assistance.

This Recommendation encourages Member countries to cooperate in this area under any other instruments, agreements, or arrangements.

RECOMMENDS that:

Member countries work to develop frameworks for closer, faster, and more efficient co-operation among their Spam Enforcement Authorities that includes, where appropriate:

a) Establishing a domestic framework.

Member countries should in this respect:

(i) Introduce and maintain an effective framework of laws, Spam Enforcement Authorities, and practices for the enforcement of Laws Connected with Spam.

(ii) Take steps to ensure that Spam Enforcement Authorities have the necessary authority to obtain evidence sufficient to investigate and take action in a timely manner against violations of Laws Connected with Spam that are committed from their territory or cause effects in their territory. Such authority should include the ability to obtain necessary information and relevant documents.

(iii) Improve the ability of Spam Enforcement Authorities to take appropriate action against (a) senders of electronic communications that violate Laws Connected with Spam and (b) individuals or companies that profit from the sending of such communications.

(iv) Review periodically their own domestic frameworks and take steps to ensure their effectiveness for cross-border co-operation in the enforcement of Laws Connected with Spam.

(v) Consider ways to improve redress for financial injury caused by spam.

b) Improving the ability to cooperate.

Member countries should improve the ability of their Spam Enforcement Authorities to cooperate with foreign Spam Enforcement Authorities.

Member countries should in this respect:

(i) Provide their Spam Enforcement Authorities with mechanisms to share relevant information with foreign authorities relating to violations of their Laws Connected with Spam upon request, in appropriate cases and subject to appropriate safeguards.

(ii) Enable their Spam Enforcement Authorities to provide investigative assistance to foreign authorities relating to violations of their Laws Connected with Spam upon request, in appropriate cases and subject to appropriate safeguards, in particular with regard to obtaining information from persons; obtaining documents or records; or locating or identifying persons or things.

(iii) Designate a contact point for co-operation under this Recommendation and provide the OECD Secretariat with updated information regarding their Laws Connected with Spam and the Spam Enforcement Authority designated as the contact point. The OECD Secretariat will keep record of this information and make it available to interested parties.

c) Improving procedures for co-operation.

Before making requests for assistance as foreseen in the previous paragraphs, Spam Enforcement Authorities should:

(i) Proceed to some preliminary investigative work to determine whether a request for assistance is warranted, and is consistent with the scope and priorities set forth by this Recommendation.

(ii) Attempt to prioritise requests for assistance and, to the extent possible, make use of common resources such as the OECD Website on spam, informal channels, existing international networks and existing law enforcement co-operation instruments to implement this Recommendation.

d) Cooperating with relevant private sector entities.

Spam Enforcement Authorities, businesses, industry groups, and consumer groups should cooperate in pursuing violations of Laws Connected with Spam. In particular, Spam Enforcement Authorities should cooperate with these groups on user education, promote their referral of relevant complaint data, and encourage them to share with Spam Enforcement Authorities investigation tools and techniques, analysis, data and trend information.

Member countries should encourage co-operation between Spam Enforcement Authorities and the private sector to facilitate the location and identification of spammers.

Member countries should also encourage participation by private sector and non-member economies in international enforcement co-operation efforts; efforts to reduce the incidence of inaccurate information about holders of domain names; and efforts to make the Internet more secure.

Where appropriate, Spam Enforcement Authorities and the private sector should continue to explore new ways to reduce spam.

INVITES non-member economies to take due account of this Recommendation and collaborate with Member countries in its implementation.

INSTRUCTS the Committee for Information, Computer and Communications Policy and the Committee on Consumer Policy to monitor the progress in cross-border enforcement co-operation in the context of this Recommendation within three years of its adoption and thereafter as appropriate.

Annex II:
BIAC and MAAWG Best Practices for Internet Service Providers and Network Ooperators[1]

Background

ISPs and network operators have an important role in the fight against spam.

Given this important role, ISPs, network operators, technical groups and alliances continue to share best practices for preventing/diminishing spam sent from or across their networks.

Although best practices will not, in and of themselves, constitute a comprehensive solution to spam, they are part of a multi-prong strategy for addressing the problem of spam. The larger the number of entities endorsing and applying common practices, the more effective they will be.

In the event that these voluntary Best Practices are taken up by ISPs and Network Operators, their positive impact will be increased if end-users also take necessary steps to protect the security of their computers, software and networks, including the protection of their personal identity on-line.

Intent

BIAC's Best Practices for ISPs and Network Operators are a set of voluntary principles developed by business aimed at enhancing the security of network infrastructures in the fight against Spam. Industry will continue to collaborate on additional technical and procedural measures to further implement these principles.

BIAC proposes the following Best Practices for ISPs and Network Operators as an important tool in combating Spam. These Best Practices and any additional measures are voluntary, and in all cases precedence is given to applicable legal and regulatory frameworks.

Implementation of these Best Practices and any additional measures will vary, depending on the technical configurations of particular providers'/operators' networks, and their specific business needs and challenges. We note that flexibility in the implementation of these Best Practices and any additional measures is the key to achieving their broad and meaningful adoption by service providers of all sizes.

1 BIAC was created in March 1962 as an independent organisation recognised by the OECD as the official representative of the OECD business community (http://www.biac.org). BIAC's members are the major industrial and employers' organisations in the 30 OECD member countries, representing over 8 million companies. Via its 31 standing committees and policy groups, BIAC mirrors all economic policy issues the OECD covers and examines their potential impacts on business in both member and an increasing number of non-member countries like Russia, China and India.

The Messaging Anti-Abuse Working Group (http://www.MAAWG.org) is a global organization focusing on preserving electronic messaging from online exploits and abuse with the goal of enhancing user trust and confidence, while ensuring the deliverability of legitimate messages. With a broad base of Internet Service Providers (ISPs) and network operators representing over 600 million mailboxes, key technology providers and senders, MAAWG works to address messaging abuse by focusing on technology, industry collaboration and public policy initiatives.

Given the rapid pace of technological change, the Best Practices will be periodically reviewed and updated.[2]

Best practices

Context/Definitions

In any given national jurisdiction, each of the Best Practices is understood to be recommended only if it is not in contradiction with existing national legislation.

In the context of these Best Practices "ISPs and network operators" include any entity operating a SMTP server connected to the Internet.

BIAC recommends to ISPs and Network Operators that:

1. Within the boundaries of the appropriate legal framework, ISPs and network operators address the problem of compromised end-user equipment by establishing timely processes to allow such end-user equipment and network elements to be managed and eliminated as sources of Spam;

2. ISPs and network operators utilize industry standard technology to authenticate their email and/or their sources;

3. ISPs and network operators block potentially infecting email file attachments. In the case of filtering email or email file attachments based on content properties, in the context of any required legislation prior agreement is to be obtained from the customer;

4. ISPs and network operators actively monitor the volume of inbound and outbound email traffic to determine unusual network activity and the source of such activity, and respond appropriately;

5. ISPs and network operators establish appropriate inter-company processes for reacting to other network operators' incident reports, also accepting end user complaints.

6. ISPs, network operators and enterprise email providers communicate their security policies and procedures to their subscribers;

7. ISPs and network operators attempt to send non-delivery notices (NDNs) only for messages originated by their own account holders;

8. ISPs and network operators take measures to ensure that only their account holders use their e-mail submit servers;

2 The Best Practices will be maintained by BIAC and MAAWG. Updated/improved versions will be available online on the MAAWG or BIAC Web sites. More information is available at www.oecd-antispam.org.

9. ISPs and network operators ensure that all domain names, Domain Name System (DNS) records and applicable Internet protocol (IP) address registration records (e.g. WHOIS, Shared WHOIS Project [SWIP] or referral WHOIS [RWHOIS]) are responsibly maintained with correct, complete and current information, and that this information includes points of contact for roles responsible for resolving abuse issues including, but not limited to, postal address, phone number and email address;

10. ISPs and network operators ensure that all their publicly routable and Internet-visible IP addresses have appropriate and up-to-date forward and reverse DNS records and WHOIS and SWIP entries; that all local area network (LAN) operators are compliant with Request for Comments (RFCs) 1918 – "Address Allocation for Private Internets," and that in particular, LANs do not use IP space globally registered to someone else, or IP space not registered to anyone, as private IP space.

Annex III:
BIAC[3] Best Practices for Email Marketing[4]

Background

This elaboration of a set of voluntary best practices for email marketing is designed to provide guidance to online marketers so that they may adopt communication techniques which are at the same time spam-free and more effective. Such rules should make clear that spam has no role to play in legitimate marketing.

Most responsible organizations already follow industry codes or have adopted best practices. This document brings together a set of voluntary best practices drawing upon existing codes in order to provide all with a basis for using email for commercial or marketing purposes.

Increasingly, Internet service providers (ISPs) and email service providers (ESPs) are looking for ways to stop spam by using filtering, black and white lists. As a result, they are inadvertently blocking legitimate email messages before they reach their intended recipients. The BIAC voluntary Best Practices for E-Mail marketing have been developed to aid business in ensuring that their own legitimate commercial email messages reach their intended recipients.

Intent

BIAC's Best Practices for Email Marketing are a set of voluntary recommendations developed by business aimed at enhancing the legitimate commercial communications on the Internet in the fight against Spam.

BIAC proposes the following Best Practices Email Marketing as an important tool in combating Spam. As these Best Practices are voluntary, in all cases precedence is given to applicable legal and regulatory frameworks. As such, they are intended to complement existing laws that govern spam, privacy, e-mail marketing and marketing to children.

As suggestions of responsible business practices related to marketing, these Best Practices are meant to represent a global business view of responsible marketing practices that protect consumer interests while enabling needed business flexibility to service customer needs and explore new types of business opportunities. BIAC is cognizant of the fact that some national/regional legal frameworks or individual business practices may be more restrictive that those suggested. BIAC in no way suggests that these recommendations should be used where they may be less stringent than legally mandated requirements.

Given the rapid pace of technological change, they will be reviewed on a periodic basis to ensure that they remain relevant to the use of the Internet as a viable communication channel for legitimate e-mail marketers.

---

3 BIAC was created in March 1962 as an independent organisation recognised by the OECD as the official representative of the OECD business community. BIAC's members are the major industrial and employers' organisations in the 30 OECD member countries, representing over 8 million companies. Via its 31 standing committees and policy groups, BIAC mirrors all economic policy issues the OECD covers and examines their potential impacts on business in both member and an increasing number of non-member countries like Russia, China and India.

4 Following the Task Force discussion BIAC is proposing to modify the wording of these best practices.

Recommended Best Practices

1. **<u>The sending of electronic commercial messages should respect the consent requirements set by the national legislation in force in the country from which the marketer is operating, unless the marketer is knowingly and intentionally targeting consumers residing in another country.</u>**

2. **<u>Organizations should keep records of opt-in/opt-out requests so that email lists can be cleaned prior to campaign broadcasts.</u>**

Organizations should ensure that they have the means to honour opt-in/opt-out requests on a timely basis and to clean their lists accordingly.

An internal process should be in place that records proof of consent, when necessary, including the date and time. Additional records with respect to the consent might include originating Internet protocol (IP) address and location (including URL), where the address collection occurred and whether consent was obtained via another medium (e.g. business card, contest form, telephone, verbal communication or credit card [e.g. through a paying subscription to a list]). Organizations should be able to provide this information to a recipient upon request provided a reasonable amount of time has passed to permit database input.

3. **<u>In all marketing email (excluding transactional mail), recipients should be provided with an obvious, clear and efficient email or web-based means to opt out of receiving any further business and/or marketing email messages from the organization.</u>**

In all email messages to current or perspective customers, organizations should include an opportunity for the recipient to opt out. This opportunity should not be buried in the email message and should, at minimum, be website- and/or email-enabled. The language used should be as simple as: "If you no longer wish to receive marketing offers from this organization, please **click here** or email **info@ABCcompany.com**."

The process for opting out should be simple and straightforward, and organizations should confirm by email or by website notice that the opt-out request has been or will be followed through without requiring further action by the consumer.

4. **<u>Every email marketing communication should clearly identify the sender of the email. The subject line and body text in the communication should accurately reflect the content, origin and purpose of the communication.</u>**

The identification of the sender and source of the email should be clearly and obviously specified and, whenever possible, placed above the fold (that part of the email that is visible without scrolling).

Example A: Direct from organization to subscriber

Date: Tue, 5 Oct 2004 07:32:02 -0400; From: Bell Canada - Electronic bill bill.presentment@bell.ca TO: JOE CONSUMER " joe@consumer.com Subject: Your Bell e-bill is ready / Votre facture électronique est prête

Example B: Third-party email service provider to subscriber on behalf of an organization

From: "peteMOSS PUBLICATIONS <bounces@peteMOSS.com>" v2user-13990-IXoyuP..CahrNet_0bkttg @mailer.whitehat.com Subject: SpamNEWS 07/21/04 To: joe@consumer.com Date: Sat, 24 Jul 2004 18:50:17 -0700

Even in cases where the content is accurately related to the subject line, organizations are cautioned against using subject lines that refer to "free offers" or "winning prizes." This is, in part, due to the fact that some spam filters use keywords such as these to signal that the message is spam.

Email messages should include the sender's main postal address. All organizations are strongly encouraged to become familiar with the provisions in their national legislation of relevant countries that address this issue.

5. **Every email should provide a link to the sender's privacy policy.**

Organizations should make the information on their online information gathering processes readily available in one comprehensive privacy policy on their websites. The privacy policy could also include information or a link to opt-out of receiving future commercial communications.

6. **Marketers, list brokers and list owners should take steps to ensure that the addresses on their email lists were obtained legally.**

Some examples of reasonable steps that an organization can take to ensure clean lists include:

- Reviewing the privacy policy of the broker/owner of the list;
- Reviewing the procedures, if any, used to obtain the email addresses.

Obtaining assurance that the e-mail addresses were collected in a manner consistent with applicable laws. Having the broker or owner sign a contract warranting that they have complied with the requirements of privacy legislation.

7. **Marketers should use a high degree of discretion in sending email marketing to children and young people in order to be sensitive to the knowledge, sophistication and maturity of this audience.**

The ways in which those under the age of majority perceive and react to email marketing communications are influenced by their age and experience, and the context in which the message is framed. For example, email marketing communications that are acceptable for teenagers will not necessarily be acceptable for younger children. The same applies for e-mail marketing of adult content, which includes material of a sexually explicit nature and material related to gaming and gambling, tobacco, alcohol, firearms and other weapons

For example, all email containing sexually explicit content should include the prefacing tag "SEXUALLY EXPLICIT", or such other language in the subject line.

While there is no way to guarantee the age of any person who signs up to an email subscriber list, when the content of an email is adult in nature, prior to sending the communication, efforts should be made to verify that the recipient is of age to legally receive and view such content, Organizations should, therefore, use discretion and sensitivity when marketing to those under the age of majority, and should seek to engage parental permission in such communications. If a marketer is knowingly targeting a particular country, companies should consult any domestic laws or requirements related to parental permission and ensure compliance with them.

8. **Organizations should have in place a complaint-handling system that is fair, effective, confidential and easy to use.**

Any complaints from individuals regarding the use of their email address should be dealt with courteously and within a reasonable time frame.

9. **Organizations may disclose the email addresses of existing consumers to third-party affiliates or within a family of companies if:**

i. they are using the addresses for purposes consistent with their collection (i.e. for marketing related to the original purchase or to provide services related to that purchase);

ii. there is an easy-to-use way to opt out of receiving further email communications.

iii. or, if they have consent to do so;

When sharing email databases within an organization or corporate family, companies should keep in mind that consumers may not understand that different brands may be owned by one company or that different companies may be related and share e-mail addresses, and thus it should be transparent to consumers why they are receiving additional, related marketing offers (e.g. under a company brand).

Technical Tips for Electronic Marketers

1. The following standard technical specifications are recommended to be adopted by sending parties:

- All servers (e.g. inbound, outbound, websites) should have reverse Domain Name System pointer (rDNS PTR) entries in DNS records, the forward and reverse DNS lookups for the host should match, and the sending machines should HELO/EHLO with this name.
- Sender Policy Framework (SPF) or Domain-key (e.g. http://spf.pobox.com, and http://antispam.yahoo.com/domainkeys) records should be published by the senders and third-party sites associated with a mailing (e.g. websites, ESPs, etc.) and kept current at all times. Adoption of technologies that are similar in nature should be considered as they develop and become standardized.
- IP addresses that are distinct from other site servers should be assigned to outbound mail servers.
- WHOIS database records for all sender domains should be kept accurate and complete.
- Role accounts (e.g. postmaster@ and abuse@) should be functional and actively monitored for all sender domains, including websites, referenced in email content.

2. Senders should attend to bounce messages as follows:

- They should promptly suppress "hard" (5xx – No such user / Mailbox unavailable, etc.) bounced addresses from all lists under their control when the total number of refusals surpasses three or more in fourteen days. If a 5xx bounce indicates spam blocking, the address may be reactivated if the spam block is removed.

- They should remove "soft" (4xx – Transient failures) bounced addresses when the total number of refusals surpasses five in consecutive campaigns from a single list, or five in aggregate from several lists within ten days.

Bounce-handling policies are explained in depth at the following sites:

- http://help.yahoo.com/help/us/mail/defer

- www.isipp.com/standards.php

- http://postmaster.info.aol.com/guidelines/bestprac.html

Annex IV:
GSM Association mobile Spam code of Practice[5] Version 1.0 February 2006

1. Executive Summary

1.1 About this document

The Mobile Spam Code of Practice ('the Code') is a voluntary non-legally binding document reflecting a commitment by operators and the GSMA to act against mobile spam and minimise the impact it has on customers.

Some of the principles and commitments within the Code are already contained in the laws of various countries. However, against a background of disparity in national legal environments, the mobile industry has identified the need to work together to adopt consistent approaches to dealing with spam and share best practice.

1.1.1 Scope

The Code applies to unsolicited communications sent via SMS and MMS and includes: commercial messages sent to customers without consent, commercial messages sent to customers encouraging them directly or indirectly to call or send a message to a premium rate number, and bulk fraudulent messages sent to customers (e.g. faking, spoofing or scam messages).

1.1.2 Purpose

Under the Code, the mobile operators that are signatories commit to:

- Include anti-spam conditions in all new contracts with third party suppliers.
- Provide a mechanism that ensures appropriate customer consent and effective customer control with respect to mobile operators' own marketing communications.
- Work co-operatively with other mobile operators to address spam issues.
- Provide customers with information and resources to help them minimise the levels and impact of mobile spam.
- Undertake other anti-spam activities to minimise the level and impact of mobile spam.
- Encourage governments and regulators to support industry.

The signatories will work in good faith to implement the commitments highlighted above and the GSMA will monitor the adoption and implementation of the Code. The GSMA and signatories to this Code of Practice will continue to examine issues associated with other types of spam and unsolicited communications and will update the Code as appropriate.

5 Any update of this version will be available on the GSMA Web site at: www.gsmworld.com.

2. The code of practice

This Code of Practice demonstrates mobile operators' commitment to fight proactively mobile spam and minimise the impact that it has on customers.

This Code of Practice applies to unsolicited communications sent via SMS and MMS (referred to as 'mobile spam') and specifically includes[6]

i) Commercial short messages or multimedia messages sent to customers without consent as required by national law (e.g. marketing messages).

ii) Commercial short messages or multimedia messages sent to customers encouraging them directly or indirectly to call or send a short message or other electronic communication to a premium rate number.

iii) Short messages or multimedia messages sent to customers in bulk and which are fraudulent (e.g. faking, spoofing or scam messages).

For the purpose of this Code of Practice, "commercial short messages or multimedia messages"[7] means SMS or MMS messages designed to promote, directly or indirectly, the goods, services or image of any person pursuing a commercial activity or exercising a regulated profession.

The mobile operators that are signatories to this Code of Practice commit to:

1. Include anti-spam conditions in all new contracts with third party suppliers. In these third party supplier contracts, conditions should include:

- A commitment to not send or initiate mobile spam.
- A commitment to respect the consent requirements set by relevant national legislation or selfregulatory mechanisms in force.
- A commitment to provide customers with obvious, clear and efficient means to opt-out of receiving further SMS or MMS marketing communications.
- Potential penalties for breaching the anti-spam commitments, including possible suspension and/or termination of contracts.

11. Provide a mechanism that ensures effective customer control with respect to mobile operators' own marketing communications via SMS or MMS, in line with consent requirements set out in national legislation.

The means of enabling consent could include providing customers with prior 'opt-in' consent mechanisms (where customers opt-in to receive communications) and/or 'optout' mechanisms (where customers are given the opportunity to opt-out of any future communications).

Operators also commit to:

- Ensure that the processes they use to obtain consent are clear and transparent and that records are kept of the type of consent obtained from customers, including how and when consent was received.

- Provide customers with obvious, clear and efficient means to opt-out of receiving further operator mobile marketing communications sent via SMS or MMS.

12 Work co-operatively with other mobile operators to investigate cases of mobile spam transmitted across networks and take action where appropriate.

13. Provide customers with information and resources to help them minimise the level and impact of mobile spam. These should include:

- Provision of information on operators' anti-spam policies, relevant legislation and local codes of practice.

- Advice on how to handle incidents of suspected spam, through their customer services contacts, in print and/or on their websites.

- Provision of mobile spam reporting facilities. For example, through their customer services contacts, website and/or via a 'shortcode' for customers to forward suspected mobile spam to.

14. Undertake activities designed to minimise the level and impact of mobile spam, including:

- Ensure that they have an anti-spam policy that prohibits the use of the mobile network for initiating or sending mobile spam.

- Review customer contracts, Terms & Conditions and/or Acceptable Use Policies, to ensure that up-to-date and relevant anti-spam conditions are included. For example, conditions indicating that complaints may be investigated (including co-operation with relevant public authorities as appropriate) and that the operator may terminate its service to a customer who originates mobile spam.

- Prioritise and investigate customer complaints regarding mobile spam, as appropriate, take action and report cases to the relevant public authorities, where appropriate.

- Monitor networks for signs of mobile spam and take proactive action to eliminate mobile spam, subject to the requirements of national legislation.

- Share information on best practice and co-operate with other mobile operators, nationally and internationally, to minimise mobile spam sent across networks. This should include considering the adoption of GSMA recommended techniques for detecting and dealing with the international transmission of fraudulent mobile spam and/or unsolicited SMS and MMS, which encourage a premium rate response and taking measures to ensure that the operators originating SMS and MMS are correctly identified *i.e.* to prevent "spoofing" of the sender's identification.

15. Encourage governments and regulators to:

- Support industry self-regulatory mechanisms.

- Support the development of responsible mobile marketing and premium rate industries. For example, through support for codes of practice that promote effective consent principles, transparency and clear pricing.

- Support investigation of spam abuses and fraud. For example, by addressing any data protection / privacy law issues or premium rate payment issues that may hamper mobile operators' ability to investigate mobile spam abuses.

- Support mobile operators in their efforts to combat mobile spam at the network level. For example, by permitting the use of network level filtering to identify and prevent mobile spam reaching customers.

- Create/support an environment that penalises those that send unsolicited SMS or MMS messages that encourage a premium rate response. For example, allow mobile operators to withhold payments to suspected mobile spam destinations, pending investigation of their spam activities by the relevant public authorities.

3. Implementation and review

The signatories to this Code of Practice will work in good faith to implement the commitments and measures listed above. Implementation timescales may vary for the different commitments and measures, depending on their technical complexity and the duration of existing contracts. The Code of Practice constitutes the intention of the GSMA and signatories to implement the measures as soon as practical in order to serve their customers interests.

The GSMA commits to:

- Monitor the adoption and implementation of the Code of Practice and the need for any further action.

- Invite signatories periodically to provide more detailed information on the effectiveness and proportionality of the measures taken.

- Assist operators in resolving inter-network mobile spam issues and in dealing with cases of persistent illegal or fraudulent activity, related to mobile spam.

Annex V:
London Action Plan/Contact Network of Spam Authorities Pro Forma for the Referral of Spam Investigations and Accompanying Guidance (Working Document)

The "Spam Complaint Referral" *pro forma* and accompanying guidance, have been created by the London Action Plan (LAP) and the EU Contact Network of Spam Authorities (CNSA).

The *pro forma* and guidance are flexible working documents to be used by spam enforcement agencies. They were created to *i*) serve as a checklist for agencies investigating and bringing cases, *ii*) ensure that the investigating agency provides adequate information in a referral/request for the receiving agency to evaluate whether pursuing action would have merit; and *iii*) establish guidelines to help members limit referrals to those that are most likely to result in successful enforcement actions.

London Action Plan/Contact Network of Spam Authorities Pro Forma for the Referral of Spam Investigations (Working Document)

**Please see accompanying guidance prior to providing the information*

1. Contact Details

From:	Referring Authority, Country	
	Contact Person, Title	
	Telephone	
	Email Address	
To:	Receiving Authority, Country	
	Contact Person, Title	
	Telephone	
	Email Address	

2. Status of investigation/ background to request

3. Confidentiality Requirements

☐ The Receiving Authority has agreed to maintain this referral as required by the Referring Authority, and any necessary documents regarding confidentiality have been completed prior to transmission of this referral.

4. Other Authorities Involved

5. Consequences of Spamming Activity

6. Known history (e.g. search engine references of the alleged spammers)?

7. Description of Spam

Category of Spam

- ☐ Phishing (forged emails from banks or other institutions asking for personal information)
- ☐ "So called" Nigerian Scam (appears to come from person in foreign country, offers to share hidden funds)
- ☐ Lottery and Other Prizes
- ☐ Pharmaceutical (vitamins, alternative health, pain killers, arthritis)
- ☐ Pharmaceutical – adult (Viagra etc)
- ☐ Body Enhancing (diet, weight loss, bodybuilding)
- ☐ Miracle Cures (AIDS, arthritis, cancer, etc.)
- ☐ Merchandise (Jewellery, watches)
- ☐ Computer software, hardware
- ☐ Mortgages, loans, financial services
- ☐ Business opportunities, work-at-home, job offers
- ☐ Pornographic content
- ☐ Online Gambling
- ☐ Dating services
- ☐ Educational, degrees, grants
- ☐ Charity (disaster appeals,etc)
- ☐ Other ____________________

Spam Details

Approximate Volume of Spam Sent	
Time Frame in Which Spam Was Sent	
Breaches of Legislation (if known)	

8. Spam Transmission Information

Attach 10 sample spam messages, if possible. Be sure to include the message's <u>extended headers</u> and complete message body, including any images.

Number of messages attached: ___________

Spam Att. #	Originating IP Address	ISP (or entity that IP address assigned to)	Contacted? Information Obtained?
1			
2			
3			
4			
5			
6			
7			
8			
9			
10			

Provide any impediments to obtaining IP user information.

Indicate whether based on available data, spam appears to be sent from any of the following:

1) open relay/proxy ☐ 2) zombie drones/botnets ☐ 3) headers appear to be forged ☐

Explanation/Basis

9. Parties Identified

Sender(s) The Sender is the entity that pays "Initiator" to spam on its behalf. Include individual or company name, physical address, website, country, telephone, email address, etc. Note if additional senders have been identified, but are not listed here.	Sender 1
	Sender 2
	Sender 3
	Sender 4
	Other Senders identified but not listed here?
Initiator(s) The Initiator is the spammer. Include individual names, physical address, country, website, telephone, email address, online usernames, aliases, etc. Note if additional initiators have been identified, but are not listed here.	Initiator 1
	Initiator 2
	Initiator 3
	Initiator 4
	Other Initiators identified but not listed here?

Physical postal address provided in the spam (if any)	
Websites, company names, or products being advertised by spam	

10. Spamvertized URLs, Purchase Page URLs, and related Whois information

Spamvertised URLS

	Spamvertised URL	Whois Information (provide payment info. if known)	Whois Source	Registrar and Country Where Domain Name Registrar Located (Contacted?)
S1				
S2				
S3				
S4				
S5				
S6				

(If applicable) Provide the reason why Domain Name Registrar was not contacted. Should Receiving Agency attempt to contact Domain Name Registrar? Is there other relevant information regarding Whois information?

Purchase Page URLS

	Purchase Page URL	Whois Information (provide payment info. if known)	Whois Source	Registrar and Country Where Domain Name Registrar Located (Contacted?)
P1				
P2				
P3				
P4				
P5				
P6				

(If applicable) Provide the reason why Domain Name Registrar was not contacted. Should the Receiving Authority attempt to contact Domain Name Registrar? Is there other relevant information regarding Whois information?

11. Additional Sources of Information

12. Other information related to URLs used

URL # from previous pages	Hosting provider/ Location of host	Information obtained (if any)	DNS provider	Information obtained (if any)
S1				
S2				
S3				
S4				
S5				
S6				
P1				
P2				
P3				
P4				
P5				
P6				

13. Email addresses used by target

	Email address	Source	ESP (Email Service Provider) contacted?	Result (information obtained, incomplete or appears fake)
1				
2				
3				
4				
5				
6				
7				
8				
9				
10				
11				
12				
13				
14				
15				

14. Forensic software used in the investigation

15. Financial data found during the investigation or deemed necessary

16. Summary of contacts made and available evidence

Using the check list below, please indicate which third-party entities have been contacted as well as whether information from such entities is either available or attached to pro forma. Please use the space provided to include the name and contact details of the organisation or person.

Entity	Entity contacted?	Evidence available?	Evidence attached?
Bank/Financial	☐	☐	☐
Domain Registrar(s)	☐	☐	☐
ISP/ESP	☐	☐	☐
Telephone company	☐	☐	☐
Postal authority	☐	☐	☐
Consumers	☐	☐	☐
Other: ____________	☐	☐	☐
Other: ____________	☐	☐	☐

London Action Plan/Contact Network of Spam Authorities Protocol for the Referral of Spam Investigations and accompanying guidance (Working Document)

Contents

Introduction

This protocol is designed to assist with the completion of the accompanying LAP/CNSA Spam Referral Template. It outlines some procedures that could greatly facilitate the referral of a spam investigation to another LAP/CNSA participating authority [or member].

Given the highly technical nature of spam investigations, a uniform referral method can greatly facilitate the referral of spam investigations to the appropriate authority. This referral method is the accompanying Spam Referral Template. The template should be completed to the fullest extent possible by the Referring Authority before referring any spam investigation to another LAP/CNSA participating authority. The main advantage of the template is that it will allow spam investigations to reach the correct authority in a uniform manner. According to its national law, the Receiving Authority can then process the information and consider pursuing the action in a timely fashion without having to do a great deal of additional investigation.

This protocol will assist you in completing the template.

Instructions for completing the template

1. Contact details

Include the contact details for your authority, the Referring Authority, and the authority to which the investigation is being referred, the Receiving Authority. See *Annex A* to this template for contact information for LAP/CNSA participating authorities.

Where there is more than one authority in any particular country, one authority will act as the main point of referral for that country.

2. Status of investigation/ background to request

Provide a brief summary of the investigation, including why the matter is being referred to the Receiving Authority. Please make it clear if the Referring Authority is taking any further action, and if co-ordinated action is required. Please mention if caution is needed in continuing the investigation due to offensive content of the spam or related internet pages (e.g. pornographic content).

3. Confidentiality requirements

Provide any procedural or evidentiary requirements impacting how the information contained in the template should be used. Additionally, indicate whether the referral or any part of the referral should be treated as confidential or used only for a specified purpose.

Prior to sending the referral, the Referring Authority should contact the Receiving Authority to determine whether the Receiving Authority will maintain the confidentiality from documents to be completed and signed by the Receiving Authority, this should be completed before the referral is made. Please check box in this section of the template to verify that any confidentiality requirements of the Referring Authority have been met.

4. Other authorities involved

Please include any other authorities that have provided assistance with the investigation.

5. Consequences of spamming activity

If known, outline the consequences or anticipated consequences of the spamming activity. This could include the number of complaints received by your agency about the spam, the number of consumers impacted, any loss of productivity caused by the spam, and the total monetary loss.

6. Known history

Please include a summary of any known history about the alleged spammers (e.g. search engine references, Rokso, blacklists, etc).

7. Description of spam

In this section, please summarize key aspects of the spam that is the subject of the referral:

- Category of the spam. Using the checkboxes, select the category or categories of spam to which the spam applies.
- Indicate the volume of spam sent.
- Indicate the time period in which the spam was sent.
- Provide the legislation that the spam appears to violate.

8. Spam transmission information

Attach to this form 10 sample spam messages, including the message's extended headers and message body. The sample spam messages may be attached on paper or in electronic format. Give each spam message an Attachment Number, and provide information about each sample spam message as requested on the template. Spam messages in addition to the 10 samples that are requested can be provided in electronic format as an attachment to the template.

The lack of copies of complete spam messages can significantly hamper the ability of a Receiving Authority to act upon a referral. The Receiving Authority can investigate and determine the identities of the sender and the initiator more easily if it has a wide sampling of messages to review.

This section solicits detailed transmission information about the spam you are attaching.

- Using the attachment numbers, for each spam message you have attached, list the IP address where the spam appears to originate. Using an IP Whois service (such as www.DNSstuff.com, Cygwin, etc) indicate the ISP (or other entity) that the IP address has been assigned to. Finally, indicate whether the ISP was contacted and if so, whether that contact resulted in additional information.

- Explain any impediments to obtaining information about the sending IP addresses, for example, if the ISP is located in another country; the ISP would not keep the request confidential; or whether the headers appeared to be forged.

- If applicable, indicate whether spam appears to be sent through an open relay or open proxy, via a zombie drone or botnet, or whether the headers appear to have been forged, and provide the basis for that determination.

9. Parties identified

Identify the parties involved in the spamming activity. For the purposes of this template, the "Sender" is the company that pays the spammer(s) to send email on its behalf, and is typically the company whose product or service is being advertised by the spam. The "Initiator" is the actual spammer who sends the spam.

- Sender(s) – list any identifying information known about the "sender," including company name, physical address, website, etc. Be sure to include the country where the sender is located. Multiple senders can be listed.

- Initiator(s) – list any identifying information known about the "sender," including name, physical address, email address, online usernames or other identities or aliases. Be sure to include the country where the initiator is located. Multiple initiators can be listed.

- Physical postal address – provide postal addresses, if any, listed in the spam.

- Company names and/or products being advertised by spam.

10. Spamvertised URLs, purchase pages, and related Whois information

The "**Spamvertised URL**" (the URL that is advertised by the spam) is the hyperlink that consumers would click if they wanted to purchase the offer being advertised by the spam. These URLs can change frequently. Many times, these URLs may redirect the consumer to a different URL where the offer or product can be purchased. The website where the offer or product can be purchased will be referred to as the "Purchase Page URL." The "Spamvertised URL" is usually a domain name registered by the "initiator" and the "**Purchase Page URL**" is usually a domain name registered to the "sender."

- In the tables, list the "Spamvertised" and "Purchase Page" URLs. In each table, codes will accompany each URL listed, where "S" will represent a Spamvertised URL and "P" will represent the Purchase Page URL. These codes will help to easily reference a particular URL throughout the template.

- List the URLs' Whois Information and any information about who paid for the domain name's registration, if that information is obtained (can require a judicial order or subpoena).

- In the "Whois Source" field, include whether the Whois information being provided was obtained from either an online Whois database (such as from www.betterwhois.com or www.whois.sc) or whether the Whois information was obtained from the Domain Name Registrar directly (such as from a subpoena).

- Provide the name and country of the Domain Name Registrar, and whether Registrar was contacted for information.

- If there are many different URLs used, provide only those with a unique domain names. Additional information related to these URLs may be attached to the Pro Forma.

- For the Spamvertised and the Purchase Page URLs, if the domain name registrar was not or could not be contacted for any reason, indicate the reason why in the text boxes provided (*i.e.* Registrar is located in another country, Registrar would not keep the request confidential, etc.). This text box can also be used for any notes about the Whois information, such as whether it appears to fake, or any other relevant information.

11. Additional Sources of Information

Provide details of any additional sources of information, which may assist with this investigation (e.g. websites, news links etc).

12. Other relevant information related to URLs used

Using the codes from the previous tables, list other information related to each URL. This would include information related to Hosting provider, where Host is located, or who provides DNS services.

13. Email addresses used by target

List the email addresses related to the spamming activity. During the course of an investigation, email addresses may be identified in places other than in the actual headers of spam messages. For example, an email address may be listed on a website or on that website's Whois information. Identification of the owners of these email addresses can help to identify the individuals behind the spam activity.

- For the "source" of the email address, identify where the email address was located (in spam, on a website (which one?), or in whois information (for which domain?).

- List whether the Email Service Provider (the "ESP") was contacted and what, if any, information was obtained from the ESP. If the email address is spammer@yahoo.com, the ESP would be Yahoo! Inc. The ESP can be contacted for additional information related to an email address. Note that free email services such as Yahoo or Hotmail may not have complete or accurate information. They do, however, record and keep for a short period of time the IP address of the computer that was used most recently to log into the email account. Using this IP address, the ISP that owns the IP address can be contacted to obtain additional information about which computer was used to log into the email account.

14. Forensic software used

Please provide a list of any forensic software that was used in the investigation (*e.g.* dd-copies, encase, etc).

15. Financial data found during the investigation

Please provide brief details of any financial data that has been gathered during the investigation or that will be needed.

16. Summary of contacts made and available evidence

Using the check list provided, indicate which third-party entities have been contacted for further information. Please provide the name of the organisation or individual, and contact details in the appropriate box. For those that were contacted, indicate whether evidence from those entities is available and whether that evidence has been attached with the template.

Notes

1 See also in Annex V the LAP/EU CNSA Spam Complaint Referral pro forma (working document) aiming to facilitate assistance requests and the referral of a spam investigation to another participating authority.

2 OECD Workshop on Spam, Brussels, Belgium, 2-3 February 2004. Background paper on line at: http://www.oecd.org/document/47/0,2340,en_2649_22555297_26514927_1_1_1_1,00.html.

3 Background reports and materials were prepared by Task Force members and by the OECD Secretariat: "Anti-Spam Regulation Report", A. Maurer, DCITA, Australia (2005); "Report on spam cross-border enforcement", J. Radish, OECD/ICCP (2004); "Anti-SPAM Initiatives: Alliances and Self Regulation", BIAC (2005); "Anti-Spam Techniques for Incoming Mail", French *Département de Développement des Média*, US Federal Trade Commission, BIAC; "Report on Education and Awareness initiatives", Mina Park, OECD (2005); "Spam Issues in Developing Countries", S. Ramasubramanian. The documents are currently available on line at: www.oecd-antispam,org.

4 "World Telecommunication Indicators 2004/2005", ITU.

5 OECD Broadband Statistics 2005, on line at: www.oecd.org/sti/telecom.

6 OECD Guidelines for the Security of Information Systems and Networks: Towards a Culture of Security http://www.oecd.org/dataoecd/16/22/15582260.pdf

7 For a definition of "phishing" see paragraphs below.

8 The SMTP envelope information is defined in: J. Klensin, "Simple Mail Transfer Protocol", IETF Network Working Group, Standards Track April 2001, http://www.ietf.org/rfc/rfc2821.txt, <accessed July 2004>. Other envelope information, the header, message body, and MIME attachments to the body are defined in: Pete Resnick, "Internet Message Format", IETF Network Working Group, Standards Track April 2001, http://www.ietf.org/rfc/rfc2822.txt <accessed July 2004>.

9 Information in this section was extracted from the Anti-Spam Research Group Discussion Archive – Date Index, http://www1.ietf.org/mail-archive/web/asrg/current/maillist.html, <accessed January 2005>.

10 Information about GSM Association is available at: http://www.gsmworld.com/index.shtml.

11 See for example "Scientists warn Skype ideal for hackers", 26 January 2006, on line at: http://today.reuters.co.uk/news/newsArticle.aspx?type=internetNews&storyID=2006-01-26T193207Z_01_L2671747_RTRIDST_0_OUKIN-UK-SECURITY-INTERNET.XML.

12 Session Initiation Protocol (SIP) is a protocol developed by the IETF (and accepted by the 3GPP in 2000 as an element of IMS architecture), which proposes a standard for initiating, modifying, and terminating an interactive user session that involves multimedia elements such as video, voice, instant messaging, online games, and virtual reality. It is one of the leading signalling protocols for Voice over IP, along with H.323. See http://en.wikipedia.org/wiki/Session_Initiation_Protocol.

13 IP Multimedia Subsystem (IMS) is a standardised Next Generation Networking (NGN) architecture for telecom operators that want to provide mobile and fixed multimedia services. See www.wikipedia.org.

14 Netcraft "October 2005 Survey", on line at: http://news.netcraft.com/

15 For more information, see the paper " The Secondary Market for Domain Name", online at http://www.oecd.org/dataoecd/14/45/36471569.pdf.

16 For more information about blogs, see the *OECD Information Technology Outlook 2006.*

17 Definition of phishing by the United States Dept. of Justice, in "Special Report on Phishing" 2004, available at: http://www.usdoj.gov/criminal/fraud/Phishing.pdf (last visited Oct. 19, 2004). See also Wikipedia definition at: http://en.wikipedia.org/wiki/Phishing.

18 See Netcraft "Phishing attacks evolved steadily through 2005", on line at: http://news.netcraft.com/archives/2005/12/29/phishing_attacks_evolved_steadily_throughout_2005.html

19 This practice is called pharming, i.e. "the exploitation of a vulnerability in the DNS server software that allows a cracker to acquire the Domain name for a site, and to redirect, for instance, that website's traffic to another web site". Wikipedia http://en.wikipedia.org/wiki/Pharming.

20 The Anti-Phishing Working Group estimates that the average life span of a phish website is 5.3 days.

21 See MessageLabs "2005 Annual Security Report", online at: http://www.messagelabs.com/. See also "Online Scammers go Spear-phishin'", *New York Times*, 04 December 2005. Pew Internet Report on Spam and Phishing, online at http://www.pewinternet.org/PPF/r/155/report_display.asp.

22 See OECD Anti-spam Task Force background paper "Spam issues in developing countries", on line at: www.oecd.org/sti/spam/toolkit.

23 Available on line (in HTML or Pdf formats) at: http://www.oecd-antispam.org/article.php3?id_article=1.

24 A more detailed analysis of the different elements included in anti-spam legislation in OECD countries, their importance, and likely impact is provided in the Anti-Spam Regulation Report. The report, as well as this section of the Toolkit, aims to aid the development and review of anti-spam regulation strategies and arrangements.

25 The European Union Directive 2002/58/EC, covers in particular "automated calling machines, telefaxes, and electronic mails, including SMS messages", but explicitly excludes person-to-person voice telephony calls, leaving the decision on how – and if – to regulate these to individual member countries. The Australian anti-spam Act is similar, though it excludes faxes, and a similar decision will probably be taken in the forthcoming New Zealand law. Japan and Korea are giving even higher attention to mobile spam, considering the large adoption of Internet-enabled mobile phones, which are used also to connect to the Internet, receive e-mails, and chat through instant messenger (IM).

26 A "Wiki" is a Web application that allows users to add content, as on an Internet forum, but also allows anyone to edit the content. See http://en.wikipedia.org/wiki/Wiki.

27 In European countries and Australia, for example, opt-in (expressed consent) is generally applied, but inferred consent is sufficient when there is an existing business relationship. In addition, many European countries adopted the opt-in approach for physical persons, but apply opt-out for messages sent to legal persons (companies, etc). This approach has been criticised as it leaves open the possibility to send unsolicited commercial messages to company's addresses, as companies argue that their e-mail addresses are easier targets for spammers. At the same time it leaves the door open for legitimate online marketers to conduct their traditional B2B activities unhindered.

28 See US National Do Not Email Registry Report, page 9, on line at: http://www.ftc.gov/reports/dneregistry/report.pdf.

29 See the FTC Report "Do Not Spam Registry", and the paper "Effectiveness and enforcement of the CAN-SPAM Act", FTC, December 2005.

30 In the context of computer software, a Trojan horse is a malicious program that is disguised as legitimate software. See http://en.wikipedia.org/.

31 The Italian criminal code, for example, sanctions behaviour such as the unauthorised access to protected computer systems, the diffusion of viruses, the damaging of computer systems and networks, etc. The US CAN-SPAM act prohibits the transmission of commercial e-mails from protected computers that have been accessed without authorization. The Act also forbids the utilisation of protected computers to relay or retransmit these e-mails, with the intent to deceive or mislead recipients – or any Internet access service – as to the origin of such messages.

32 The French legislation provides a good example of a comprehensive approach to spam and all related problems, such as cybersecurity and consumer protection. The "Loi 2004-575 pour la confiance dans l'économie numérique" includes provisions which modify at the same time the Consumer protection law, telecommunication regulation, and the criminal code, inserting specific wording to deal with spam, deceptive or illegal content, cybercrime, cryptography, etc. With the *"Loi pour la Confiance dans l'Economie Numérique,"* the French government streamlined, linked and updated existing instruments in a coherent and inclusive manner to face new challenges and unexpected technological evolutions.

33 The convention entered into force in July 2004. For the moment only 10 countries ratified the text, which has otherwise been signed by 32 countries, including non-European countries such as Canada, South Africa, United States and Japan. See also the 2005 EU Framework Decision on attacks against information systems: 2005/222/JHA, OJ No L 69, 16 March 2005.

34 The US CAN-SPAM act refers to "multiple" messages when considering aggravated violations such as e-mails sent through a protected computer without authorisation. CAN-SPAM Act of 2003, Section 4.

35 The Australian Spam Act of 2003, for example, establishes that the legislation is applicable to all messages having an "*Australian link*", *i.e.* originating from Australia, or from individuals or organisations physically present in Australia or from an organisation whose central management and control is in Australia, etc (Section 7, Spam Act 2003). Similar provisions are included in European anti-spam legislation, such as the Dutch Telecommunication Act, which gives OPTA (the telecommunication regulator) the possibility to take actions against spammers based in the Netherlands, or operating from the country, or if the products advertised are sold from a Netherlands-based company, etc.

36 Collective action can be particularly useful in cases where large numbers of consumers have each suffered small losses. It offers an avenue for redress to consumers who, due to the low value of the claim, would not be willing to undertake the burden and cost of legal action individually. See OECD Workshop on Consumer Dispute Resolution and Redress in the Global Marketplace, Background Report, April 2005. On line at: www.oecd.org/sti/consumer-policy.

37 For example in Australia these industry codes can be registered by the national communication Authority (the ACA). Registration enables the ACA to require an industry participant to comply with the code, enforcing its provisions in case the industry association fails to do so.

38 See Australian Telecommunication Act 1997 (amended), sections 112 and 113.

39 See the Report on Anti-Spam Law Enforcement (www.oecd-antispam.org) which provides an analysis of the current situation and a series of recommendations to improve cross-border enforcement activities.

40 About the status of implementation of the directive, see the EC communication on line at: http://europa.eu.int/information_society/topics/ecomm/doc/all_about/implementation_enforcement/annualreports/10threport/sec20041535VOL1en.pdf.

41 Spam Act 2003, on line at: http://scaleplus.law.gov.au/html/pasteact/3/3628/top.htm

42 United States: "Controlling the Assault of Non-Solicited Pornography and Marketing Act"- 117 Stat. 2699 Public Law 108- 187- Dec. 16, 2003, on line at: http://frwebgate.access.gpo.gov/cgibin/useftp.cgi?IPaddress=162.140.64.88&filename=publ187.108&directory=/diskb/wais/data/108_cong_public_laws. Korea: "Act on Promotion of Information and Communication and Communications Network Utilization and Information Protection" (2001) and revised act of 2002, on line at:http://www.spamcop.or.kr/eng/m_2.html

43 See M. Geist "Untouchable?: A Canadian perspective on the anti-spam battle", on line at: http://www.michaelgeist.ca/geistspam.pdf

44 Discussion paper "Legislating against spam", IT & Telecommunications Policy Group, Ministry of Economic Development, New Zealand. On line at:http://www.politechbot.com/docs/new.zealand.spam.051804.pdf

45 The government's proposed law was announced on 24 February 2004. Online information: http://www.med.govt.nz/pbt/infotech/spam/index.html

46 See OECD Table of Cases, annex B, OECD Report on Anti-Spam Law Enforcement, on line at: www.oecd-antispam.org.

47 The Australian Spam Act establishes that in determining the peculiar penalty, the court must have regard to all relevant matters, including: the nature and extent of the contravention and of any loss or damage suffered as a result of the contravention, as well as the circumstances in which the contravention took place; whether the person has previously been found by the Court in proceedings under this Act to have engaged in any similar conduct. See Spam Act 2003, Sec. 24, at http://scaleplus.law.gov.au/html/pasteact/3/3628/top.htm

48 However caution should be exercised in imposing a regime where a penalty is imposed for each and every breach as a single spammer may send millions of messages in a single day, thereby resulting in unfeasibly large penalties.

49 *Conférence administrative des postes et télécommunications des pays d'expression française (CAPTEF), Réseau francophone de la régulation des télécommunications (FRATEL) and Institut francophone des nouvelles technologies de l'information et de la formation (INTIF).*

50 European Commission Resources on spam: http://europa.eu.int/information_society/policy/ecomm/todays_framework/privacy_protection/spam/index_en.htm.

51 The guidance and pro forma were adopted by the LAP as a referral tool in February 2006.

52 The text of the Recommendation is available in Annex I: "OECD Recommendation of the Council on cross-border co-operation in the enforcement of laws against spam".

53 To facilitate co-operation the OECD set up a contact list of enforcement agencies, which is currently being extended to cover also non-OECD member economies.

54 A "pink contract" is a contract whereby the spammer agrees to pay a fixed fee for the junk e-mail they send through the ISPs mail servers and the ISP agrees to allow the sending. It seems it gets the name pink contract from the colour of the famous tinned meat that junk e-mail is named after.

55 Email Submission between independent networks, on line at: http://www.ietf.org/internet-drafts/draft-hutzler-spamops-04.txt.

56 Anti-Spam Technical Alliance Technology and Policy Proposal, on line at: http://www.google.com/url?sa=U&start=3&q=http://docs.yahoo.com/docs/pr/pdf/asta_soi.pdf&e=9797 or http://postmaster.info.aol.com/asta/ or http://www.microsoft.com/presspass/press/2004/jun04/06-22ASTAPR.asp.

57 Botnet is a jargon term for a collection of software robots, or bots, which run autonomously. A botnet's originator can control the group remotely, usually through a means such as IRC, and usually for nefarious purposes. A botnet can comprise a collection of cracked machines running programs (usually referred to as worms, Trojan horses, or backdoors) under a common command and control infrastructure. Botnets are often used by spammers to send their e-mails.

58 See also *OECD Guidelines for the Security of Information Systems and Networks: Towards a Culture of Security*, OECD 2002, on line at:http://www.oecd.org/document/42/0,2340,en_2649_34255_15582250_1_1_1_1,00.html "Three ways phishers are hooking you", 24 May 2005, online at http://searchsecurity.techtarget.com/originalContent/0,289142,sid14_gci1090307,00.html. This is also the view expressed by S. Ramabrasubramanian in the OECD Report on Spam Issues in Developing Countries.

59 See, for example, Microsoft Anti-Spam policy at: http://privacy.msn.com/anti-spam/, Yahoo Terms of Service http://docs.yahoo.com/info/terms/, Tiscali (in Italian) http://abbonati.tiscali.it/pop-up/internet-gratis/condizioni_contrattuali.html, French ISPs association (in French) – *Association française des fournisseurs d'accès à Internet et de services en ligne* (AFA): http://www.afa-france.com/deontologie.html.

60 MAAWG Code of Conduct: http://www.maawg.org/about/CodeofConduct.pdf.

61 See http://www.spamdailynews.com/publish/index.asp.

62 FTC Operation Spam Zombies: http://www.ftc.gov/bcp/conline/edcams/spam/zombie/

63 "Stopping Spam: Creating a Stronger, Safer Internet", report of the Canadian task force on spam. Available at: http://e-com.ic.gc.ca/epic/internet/inecic-ceac.nsf/en/h_gv00317e.html.

64 http://www.maawg.org/port25.

65 See also "Best Practices for Businesses to Avoid Being Phished", Developed by the Anti-Phishing Working Group, the Mail Anti-Abuse Working Group, and the US Homeland Security Identity Theft Technology Consortium, November 2005. On line at:https://antiphishing.kavi.com/events/2005_11_fallconferencenotes/20051108_BestPracticesWorkingDoc.pdf. See also R. Rasmussen " Phishing Prevention: Making Yourself a Hard Target", and "Online Identity Theft: Phishing Technology, Chokepoints and Countermeasures" at: www.antiphishing.org/Phishing-dhs-report.pdf.

66 See EuroISPA Web site at http://www.euroispa.org/.

67 See M. Rotert presentation at the OECD Task Force meeting, on line at: http://www.oecd.org/dataoecd/52/5/34594094.pdf

68 On line at: http://www.antiphishing.org

69 Direct Marketing Association Web site: http://www.the-dma.org/

70 See press release "Vodafone K.K. adopts anti-spam measure for SMS", on line at: http://www.vodafone.com/assets/files/en/E-NoticeAnti-spamSMS.pdf

71 MMA Code for responsible mobile marketing: A code of conduct and guidelines to best practice. Online at http://www.mmaglobal.co.uk/imgs/MMA-Code-of-Conduct_Dec03.pdf

72 More information about MMA is available at: www.mmaglobal.com

73 GSM Association, http://www.gsmworld.com/using/public_policy/mobile_content.shtml; UK code of practice for the self-regulation of new forms of content on mobile, on line at: www.imcb.org.uk/assets/documents/10000109Codeofpractice.pdf and "Insights into Mobile Spam", on line at: http://www.mobilespam.org/. See also Vodafone spam policy: http://www.vodafone.com/section_article/0,3035,CATEGORY_ID%253D30407%2526LANGUAGE_ID%253D0%2526CONTENT_ID%253D265596,00.html

74 This section is the result of a preliminary study carried out by the French anti-spam contact group. It was developed by different actors, including Internet experts and civil society representatives. The study was then enhanced thanks to the contributions of BIAC and of the US before being contributed to the OECD Task Force.

75 This section presents a variety of technologies by type or category and at times may highlight a specific application in a category; this is not by way of endorsement but merely to illustrate the example. In addition, considering the rapid development of technologies, this section should be taken for an overview of technical measures available at the time of its preparation (second quarter 2005).

76 An e-mail which pretends to come from someone that has never actually been involved.

77 This section is based on the background paper on "Education and Awareness initiatives", Mina Park, OECD (2005).

78 The marginal cost for spammers to send an e-mail is so small, a return rate of only 0.025% or less is sufficient enough for a spammer to make a return on investment.

79 A survey conducted by The Pew Internet & American Life Project in March 2004 reports that 9% of e-mailers said they had responded to an e-mail that they later discovered was fraudulent, 3% had provided personal information in response to an unsolicited e-mail, and 5% of users had ordered a product or service in response to unsolicited e-mail. The IPSOS Trend Report Canada for May-June 2004 reported that more than one third of online Canadians open their spam e-mails, out of curiosity.

80 On line at: http://stopspamhere.ca/

81 On line at: http://www.iia.net.au/spamvt.html

82 Safer Internet Programme on line at: www.saferinternet.org.

83 For example the Federal Trade Commission in the US created an e-card providing users with tips about how to avoid phishing scams. The card is available on line at:http://www.ftc.gov/bcp/conline/ecards/phishing/index.html.

84 Based on OECD Guidelines for Staff Members.

85 On line at: http://www.iia.net.au/

86 More information about the Canadian Task Force is available on line at: http://e-com.ic.gc.ca/epic/internet/inecic-ceac.nsf/en/h_gv00248e.html

87 Signal-spam: http://www.signal-spam.fr.

88 See *Direction du Développement des médias*: http://www.ddm.gouv.fr/rubrique.php3?id_rubrique=63

89 SpotSpam was supported by EU communication 2004/28.

90 http://www.londonactionplan.org/

91 "Operation spam zombies", see FTC press release: http://www.ftc.gov/opa/2005/05/zombies.htm/.

92 See DDSI "Roadmap: public-private partnerships", November 2002, on line at: http://www.ddsi.org/Documents/final%20docs/ DDSI_D3_PPP_Roadmap_f.pdf.

93 This element is closely linked to the other Toolkit elements, such as technical solutions and industry-driven initiatives.

94 Regarding the inaccuracy of contact information for registered domain names, see US GAO "Internet Management: Prevalence of False Contact Information for Registered Domain Names", on line at: http://www.gao.gov/docsearch/abstract.php?rptno=GAO-06-165

95 MessageLabs Security Report 2005. On line at www.messagelabs.com

96 Pew Internet and American Life Project: http://www.pewinternet.org/PPF/r/155/report_display.asp

97 VerigSign, Internet Security Intelligence Briefing, Nov. 2004, v. 2, issue 2, at 5-6, available at: http://www.verisign.com/static/017574.pdf

98 Data are based on the number of mailboxes of each participant ISPs. In case only the number of subscribers is provided, it will be estimated that there are 1.5 mailboxes per subscriber.

99 In case new participants join the Program, they are requested to provide data starting from October 2005 in order to ensure coherence.

100 Background paper "Spam issues in developing countries", available at www.oecd-antispam.org

OECD PUBLICATIONS, 2, rue André-Pascal, 75775 PARIS CEDEX 16
PRINTED IN FRANCE
(93 2006 06 1 P) ISBN 92-64-02716-5 – No. 55247 2006